DANVILLE PUBLIC LIBRARY

W9-AZG-876

OPPORTUNITIES

in

Social Science Careers

WITHDRAWN

REVISED EDITION

PUBLIC LIBRARY
DANVILLE, ILLINOIS

ROSANNE J. MAREK

VGM Career Books

*Chicago   New York   San Francisco   Lisbon   London   Madrid   Mexico City
Milan   New Delhi   San Juan   Seoul   Singapore   Sydney   Toronto*

The *McGraw·Hill* Companies

Library of Congress Cataloging-in-Publication Data

Marek, Rosanne J.
    Opportunities in social science careers / by Rosanne Marek. — Rev. ed.
            p.   cm. (VGM opportunities series)
    ISBN 0-07-141167-4
    1. Social sciences—Vocational guidance—United States.   I. Title.
II. Series.

    H62.5.U5M37   2004
    300'.23'73—dc22   2003025822

*To my parents, Helen and James E. Marek, who taught
me that life involves far more than just earning a living; to
my sisters, Cecile and Jane, who are also my dearest friends;
and to my nephews, Michael and Ian, who have shown me
how joyous aunthood can be.*

Copyright © 2004 by The McGraw-Hill Companies, Inc. All rights reserved. Printed in the
United States of America. Except as permitted under the United States Copyright Act of
1976, no part of this publication may be reproduced or distributed in any form or by
any means, or stored in a database or retrieval system, without the prior written
permission of the publisher.

1 2 3 4 5 6 7 8 9 0   LBM/LBM   3 2 1 0 9 8 7 6 5 4

ISBN 0-07-141167-4

Interior design by Rattray Design

McGraw-Hill books are available at special quantity discounts to use as premiums and
sales promotions, or for use in corporate training programs. For more information,
please write to the Director of Special Sales, Professional Publishing, McGraw-Hill,
Two Penn Plaza, New York, NY 10121-2298. Or contact your local bookstore.

This book is printed on acid-free paper.

Contents

Foreword   vii

Preface   ix

1. What Are the Social Sciences?   1

The broad scope of social sciences. Careers in the next century.

2. Anthropology   5

Major branches of anthropology. Employment opportunities. Salaries and earnings. Preparing for a career in anthropology. Sources of additional information.

3. Sociology   15

Major branches of sociology. Sociologists study change. Careers in sociology. Related careers.

PUBLIC LIBRARY
DANVILLE, ILLINOIS

Employment opportunities. Salaries and earnings.
Preparing for a career in sociology. Sources of
additional information.

4. Psychology   27

Major branches of psychology. Related careers.
Employment opportunities. Salaries and earnings.
Preparing for a career in psychology. Sources of
additional information.

5. History   41

Major branches of history. Careers in history. Related
careers. Employment opportunities. Salaries and
earnings. Preparing for a career in history. Sources of
additional information.

6. Geography   53

Major branches of geography. Careers in geography.
Related careers. Employment opportunities. Salaries
and earnings. Preparing for a career in geography.
Sources of additional information.

7. Political Science   61

Major branches of political science. Careers in
political science. Related careers. Employment
opportunities. Salaries and earnings. Preparing for a
career in political science. Sources of additional
information.

8. Economics   71

Major branches of economics. Careers in economics. Related careers. Employment opportunities. Salaries and earnings. Preparing for a career in economics. Sources of additional information.

9. Teaching and the Social Sciences   79

The social studies in elementary, secondary, and high schools. Preparing for a career in teaching. Salaries and earnings. Employment opportunities. Teaching the social sciences in colleges and universities. Sources of additional information.

10. A Final Word About Social Science Careers   97

Career prerequisites. The changing world of work. Choosing a college or university. Conclusion.

Appendix A: Offices of Teacher Certification in the United States and Its Territories   107
Appendix B: Offices of Teacher Certification in Canadian Provinces and Territories   121
Appendix C: Selected Professional Journals in the Social Sciences   125
Resources   129

FOREWORD

SINCE THE EMERGENCE of civilization more than five millennia ago, thoughtful people of every era have proposed various social theories to explain the relationship between human beings and society; however, the social sciences are relatively new. In the aftermath of the Age of Reason, the methods of physical science came to be applied to disparate disciplines, some of which were ancient in origin and others new upon the scene in the nineteenth century. These disciplines, which deal with aspects of society or forms of social activity, we call the social sciences. As Rosanne J. Marek points out, "It is the social sciences that enable us to look beyond facts to values." Furthermore, "It is they that encourage us to aspire to knowledge and ultimately to wisdom." These disciplines include anthropology, sociology, psychology, history, geography, political science, and economics, all of which are discussed in this very useful book, together with a chapter on teaching and the social sciences.

In these difficult times, students need as much assistance as possible in choosing a career and finding a job. In this revised edition of *Opportunities in Social Science Careers*, Rosanne J. Marek provides this help by succinctly describing each discipline and discussing employment opportunities, salaries, and educational requirements for each field. Each chapter also includes a list of organizations to which students can write for additional information. Included in this revised edition are Canadian professional organizations and certification offices as well. The concluding chapter offers an excellent overview of careers in the social sciences, careers that can be extremely fulfilling. As Dr. Marek notes, those who choose such careers "are, after all, striving to be truly human." This is the great task of us all, and there can be no greater satisfaction.

John E. Weakland, Former Editor
International Journal of Social Education

PREFACE

ON THE SURFACE, it might seem odd to see the words "social" and "science" paired together. To describe "social" in its simplest terms, *Webster's* uses phrases such as "pleasant companionship with one's friends and associates." Most of us probably conjure images of being with friends in a relaxed environment, laughing and talking. What's so scientific about that? Well, reading a little further in *Webster's* we come to this: "Of or relating to human society, the interaction of the individual and the group, or the welfare of human beings as members of society." This is beginning to sound more serious and more structured than an easy friendship. You might say it's beginning to sound more scientific.

Loosely defined, science is knowledge of general truths, and it involves the means for discovering these general truths. Keeping this definition in mind, then, it is easier to see how a scientific method could be applied to study the relationships among similar or disparate groups of people. We do this not only to understand those individuals and groups themselves, but also to apply what we learn to other individuals and groups and societies, and thus, per-haps, gain greater understanding of our world.

In the natural sciences, scientists have long been accustomed to applying the scientific method to study a phenomenon. Observation and a hypothesis lead to controlled experiments that will either prove or disprove a theory in a very specific way. During this process, a number of interesting observations are made, and repeated experiments should—given the exact same conditions—yield the same results. Not necessarily so with human beings, who at any given moment and for any number of reasons will offer a different result. Time and space greatly affect how individuals, groups, and/or societies will react. It is for this reason that the seven fundamental disciplines of anthropology, sociology, psychology, history, geography, political science, and economics must be taken into account when we try to observe and explain the behavior of people.

Within the seven disciplines, there are many overlapping and interrelated roles that a social scientist can play. Here is just a small sample of what some social scientists do:

Anthropology
- Live among the members of a diminishing Native American tribe to learn their customs and record their language
- Amass, count, summarize, and interpret census data
- Get funding for and work on a neighborhood improvement project

Sociology
- Collect data to find solutions for crime, poverty, and other social problems in a given community

- Conduct public opinion polls to determine if a community could support integrated housing
- Find out how new members are recruited into street gangs in an effort to curb the growth of gangs

Psychology
- Examine the behavior of six-year-olds in a "laboratory" of six classrooms to find out why some children are more shy than others
- Work as a counselor in a large corporation, helping employees find resources to help them with stress management
- Administer standardized psychological testing to special education students in a middle school

History
- Work as a writer or editor for a publisher of high school history textbooks
- Serve as a curator of textiles for a large museum
- Help a motion picture company authenticate the visual details of a movie set in Paris in the 1940s

Geography
- Take aerial photographs of a remote region, and then create a map
- Study past earthquakes to predict future earthquakes in the western United States
- Spend a year at a base camp in Greenland tracking the shrinking of the ice sheet that covers much of it

Political Science
- Work as a political commentator for a television news station
- Run for a political office in your community
- Become a political fund-raiser

Economics
- Conduct market research surveys to determine consumer interest in a new antibacterial laundry detergent
- Evaluate a new business proposal to determine if it is eligible for a small business loan
- Research the viability of transferring your company's manufacturing division to another location

We are no longer—any of us—isolated in our own countries, communities, or homes. "Global marketplace," "global economy," "World Wide Web," and many similar terms are commonplace and illustrate how, despite great distances, we can quickly and easily connect with virtually anyone, anywhere, anytime. Today, our neighbors are halfway across the world, and like any good neighbor, it makes sense to find ways to optimize these relationships for the comfort, betterment, and security of all. The increasing interdependence of all countries of the world demands that alliances and relationships among disparate peoples, often of vastly differing cultures, be forged. Knowledgeable and dedicated social scientists are needed to help achieve these goals.

The assistance of several persons in the completion of this book is gratefully acknowledged. Chief among them are Joan Ouano Erasga, who compiled much of the data for this revised edition; Jack E. Ihle, a psychologist at the university's Counseling and Psychological Services Center; and the Career Services staff at Ball State University, especially Mridula Jarial, coordinator of its Resource Center.

1

WHAT ARE THE
SOCIAL SCIENCES?

SCIENTIFIC TECHNOLOGY HAS enabled us to fly higher and faster than birds and to swim deeper and farther than fish, but it has not taught us to walk the earth as rational human beings. While science and technology have given us the goods we need to make life more comfortable, the humanities and social sciences can give us the understanding we need to make life more worthwhile.

Knowledge is usually divided into three broad areas: the natural sciences, the humanities, and the social sciences. Natural scientists study natural objects in the universe. The disciplines of physics, chemistry, biology, astronomy, and mathematics are usually considered to be part of the natural sciences. The humanities are disciplines that use historical, critical, or philosophical approaches to knowledge. The humanities consist of language, literature, art history, music history, philosophy, religion, and sometimes, history.

Social scientists study humans, their culture, and their relationship to their environment. Social scientists often study human behavior and institutions using methods similar to those used to study the natural sciences. They gather and analyze quantitative data; that is, they try to measure statistically the phenomenon they are studying. Whether the social sciences are truly "sciences" has been an issue of debate.

The social sciences are interdisciplinary, overlapping the humanities and natural sciences. For example, some subfields, like experimental psychology and physical anthropology, overlap with biology. History is considered by some scholars to be part of the humanities. Like natural scientists, many researchers in the social sciences must write grant proposals to government agencies and foundations for funding to support their research.

The focus of this book is on career opportunities in the social sciences. Seven fields of study—history, geography, economics, political science, sociology, anthropology, and psychology—are recognized as the social sciences. Although they differ from each other in their purpose and scope, they share one essential component: Each studies individuals and their relationship with each other and their environment. Indeed, the Latin origins of the term *social sciences* can be translated as knowledge about human beings as companions, that is, social beings.

History and geography are very old disciplines, dating back to the Hebrews and Greeks. The other social sciences are relatively new fields. Most of them date their beginnings to the late nineteenth century.

The Broad Scope of Social Sciences

The total human experience is the source of content for the social sciences. In the following chapters, each of the seven disciplines is examined. Some chapters also look at statistics, since this is an important method used in the social sciences. Selected careers in each field are identified, information concerning the training and education required for each is listed, and salary ranges for various jobs are provided.

Careers in the social sciences are important to society. Those who select one of the careers outlined in this book have chosen to work in a discipline that attempts to make the world a better place. We marvel that human beings have traveled to the moon and returned safely to earth. Yet we recognize that, unfortunately, one cannot walk in safety on the streets of many of our cities at night and that some of our children lack basic literacy skills. As long as these situations exist, there is a need for the social sciences. It is the special mission of social scientists to improve the quality of life for humankind, both now and for later generations.

Careers in the Next Century

In a 1996 address in Ashland, Kentucky, President Bill Clinton observed that in five years the youth of today would have job opportunities that currently didn't exist. Indeed, there are jobs today that were unheard of a decade ago. The technology explosion has changed the world of work. Some skills, competencies, and proficiencies needed today differ vastly from those of an earlier time. This fact, coupled with the reality that most of today's college students will change jobs an estimated seven times during their lifetimes, requires the development of transferable skills such as planning, organizing, analyzing, and evaluating. These are all skills that are acquired in the study of the social sciences.

2

ANTHROPOLOGY

THE TERM *ANTHROPOLOGY* is derived from two Greek words that, taken together, mean "the study of humankind." Anthropologists study peoples and cultures of the world, past and present. They focus on the origins of human life and the physical characteristics of different peoples. Anthropologists investigate the social structures, traditions, languages, and beliefs of people throughout the world. The central issue in anthropology is human variation.

Major Branches of Anthropology

There are four major specialties in the field of anthropology. Two of them, physical anthropology and linguistics, are related not only to the social sciences but also to the life and behavioral sciences. Archaeology is related to the humanities. The fourth field, cultural anthropology, is the one most clearly identified as a social science.

Cultural anthropologists examine all phases of human life. They study the rites of initiation into a society. They are, therefore, interested in infant baptism in Christianity and the ceremonies associated with birth in African kingdoms. Anthropologists also study rites of passage from childhood to adolescence. They are interested in the study of dating, courtship, and marriage rituals.

Cultural anthropologists investigate cultural patterns and behaviors concerning death. They study the burial customs of peoples past and present. For example, when the remains of an early man were found, there were indications that flowers had been buried with him. Cultural anthropologists use evidence like those flowers to learn more about religious beliefs.

The discovery of the tomb of Tutankhamen, king of Egypt from around 1370 to 1352 B.C., helped cultural anthropologists learn much about life in ancient Egypt. They were able to determine what kinds of foods the ancient Egyptians ate, the games they played, and their favorite leisure activities. They learned about Egyptian clothing, political institutions, and beliefs about the afterlife.

Archaeology

Archaeologists study peoples and cultures from the past by the systematic recovery of material evidence, such as tools. Archaeologists use artifacts and other buried remains to study those who lived before us and reconstruct past ways of life. Archaeologists excavate, salvage, and preserve materials recovered in archaeological digs. They work outside in all kinds of weather. Archaeology has outgrown its *Raiders of the Lost Ark* image and has a scientific basis.

A fascinating newer branch of archaeology is marine archaeology. Marine archaeologists study sunken ships and ancient cities that have disappeared beneath the sea. Currently there are several exciting projects being conducted in marine archaeology. These studies are providing us with an understanding of goods traded between nations and of life onboard ships many years ago.

One of the most interesting marine expeditions lasted nearly twenty years. Margaret Rule, one of the world's leading marine archaeologists, directed the excavation and raising of King Henry VIII's flagship, the *Mary Rose*, in 1982. This ship sank in 1545 as it sailed to fight the Spanish Armada. Centuries later, marine archaeologists found the ship and its contents in the waters of Portsmouth harbor in England. Visitors to Portsmouth today can see King Henry's flagship on display.

Today's technology enables more sophisticated marine expeditions than ever before. While some of the recovery of sunken ships is done by treasure hunters who are looking for the gold or other valuable cargo the ships carried, these companies, too, are hiring archaeologists to plot out the site and recover items of historical interest. Marine archaeologists are learning much about those who lived centuries ago.

Linguistics

Linguistic anthropologists study the role of language in various cultures. They study and describe the dialects, speech patterns, and languages spoken by people throughout the world. Linguistic anthropologists are interested in languages spoken both by people who are living now and by those who lived in the past. They often travel to remote areas to study languages that are in danger of disappearing. Some of these languages have no written form and are recorded for the first time by linguists. Some linguists study animal communication for insights into human language.

Physical Anthropologists

Physical anthropologists study the evolution of the human body. They look for the first evidences of human life. Physical anthropology is sometimes called biological anthropology. It includes the study of human fossils. Physical anthropologists investigate the lives of primitive beings by studying teeth markings and bone structures. They study the genetics of human populations to learn about their history of movement and intermarriage.

Cultural Anthropology

Most anthropologists specialize in cultural anthropology. They study the customs, culture patterns, and social lives of groups. Historically, anthropologists studied non-Western cultures. Today they are as interested in people who live in modern urban cultures such as New York City as they are in those who live in relative isolation in New Guinea. Cultural anthropologists study the similarities and differences between cultures, looking for universals that underlie human diversity. Specialties within cultural anthropology include such fields as medical anthropology, which is a comparative study of health and disease.

Fieldwork

An important part of each one of these four branches of anthropology is fieldwork. Taking part in an archaeological dig is one example of fieldwork. Another example is living in a different culture to study the daily lives or language of the people. Anthropologists must have the ability to live in a culture that is very different from their own, often under primitive circumstances. Another example of fieldwork is working with the collections in a museum of natural history.

Employment Opportunities

With one exception, the largest percentage of anthropologists are employed by colleges and universities. They instruct undergraduate and graduate students. Others engage in research projects funded by foundations or other granting agencies.

The federal government employs an estimated eight hundred archaeologists. The National Park Service, for example, employs archaeologists to excavate and interpret ruins. In the field of archaeology, the largest number of jobs is in contract archaeology, also called public archaeology or cultural resource management. Recent legislation has created employment opportunities in this field. The federal government, many states, and some cities now require that whenever construction is taking place on public land or with public money, an archaeological survey must be performed first. This means that when a road is being built, an oil well drilled, or a new dam being erected, archaeologists must make sure there are no ancient remains that would be destroyed by the construction. Sometimes this work is done by the staff of a government agency such as the Bureau of Land Management, but more often it is contracted out to a university or a company that specializes in archaeology. When an important site is discovered, sometimes the development can be changed to protect it. For example, the course of a road may be moved. Other times, for instance when a dam will flood a large area, archaeologists excavate the site and remove valuable artifacts. There are now more archaeologists working in contract archaeology than in colleges and universities.

Related Careers

There are many careers related to anthropology. Included are positions in medical research, urban and regional planning, and public health. Service in the government agencies AmeriCorps and the Peace Corps is also good experience for someone interested in the field of anthropology. Some students study anthropology before entering careers in international business or public administration.

Many students who study anthropology choose careers in museums of natural history, history, or anthropology. Those who are employed by museums interpret the meaning of historic, artistic, or scientific significance of the objects housed in those museums. Some of the jobs to be found in museums that require training in anthropology are:

Curators

All objects in the museum's collections must be registered and either displayed or stored. Museum employees called curators assign catalog numbers for each group of museum objects. They also acquire artifacts, design exhibitions, and edit exhibition catalogs.

Conservation Technicians

Once an object is made part of the museum's collection, it must be maintained by the museum's staff. Objects must be kept safe from harm. Each of them requires very specific methods of preservation. Museums employ conservation technicians who take care of the items in the collection and restore and repair them. The field of museum conservation has become a highly specialized one.

Education Directors

This position requires both knowledge of the museum's collection and skills in teaching the museum's visitors about it. Education directors arrange tours and develop audiovisual programs about the collection. They schedule demonstrations and lectures for those visiting the museum, including school groups.

Growth Areas

There is expected to be modest growth in teaching positions in colleges and universities as faculty members retire. There will be little growth in government jobs, as efforts to shrink the federal and state governments continue. Jobs for museum curators and conservators are expected to increase about as fast as average for all occupations through 2010. Opportunities continue to grow for contract archaeologists in certain parts of the country.

Salaries and Earnings

According to the Bureau of Labor Statistics, the average salary for an anthropologist is $41,800. Entry-level positions in college teaching in anthropology pay around $37,000 for the academic year.

Some positions in anthropology with the federal government have pay ranges from $27,000 to $45,000, depending on the level of education. Top positions in anthropology offer salaries in excess of $60,000. They are, however, usually reserved for those with a doctorate in anthropology.

Earnings in business and industry vary widely, but they are usually about 35 percent higher than those in colleges and universities.

Museum curators have average salaries of $31,460, although administrative positions in large museums have much higher salaries. Museum curators with the federal government average $64,600 a year.

Preparing for a Career in Anthropology

If you are interested in studying anthropology, there are several high school courses that will help you. In addition to mathematics and

English composition, classes in biology and history are beneficial. A course in the use of computers is highly recommended because anthropologists today conduct research using them.

Since fieldwork experience is critical for a career in anthropology, an excellent entry point for someone interested in working as an anthropologist is work in a museum. Museums frequently have gift shops staffed by volunteers. Many museums employ interns as docents or guides. Some living museums such as Old Sturbridge Village in Massachusetts and Conner Prairie Pioneer Settlement in Indiana employ interpreters. They play the roles of historical persons and interpret the history of the times.

High school and college students interested in archaeology should consider a volunteer position with an archaeological dig during the summer. Opportunities range from the Center for American Archaeology in southern Illinois to positions with the National Forest Service and digs in foreign countries. Further information about volunteer activities can be found at museum.state.il/ismdepts /anthro/dlcfaq.html.

Educational Requirements

Entry-level positions in the field of anthropology require a bachelor's degree and some fieldwork experience. In addition to beginning courses in cultural and physical anthropology and archaeology, courses in psychology, geography, sociology, history, and physiology are useful. Students of cultural anthropology will benefit from some time spent in another culture, especially a non-Western one. Participation in a study abroad program or the Peace Corps will be useful preparation for a graduate program.

Graduate work in anthropology is required for all teaching positions at the college and university level. Most professional anthropologists have postgraduate degrees in their field. Careers in conservation archaeology or medical anthropology require graduate degrees. Those who administer projects in contract archaeology must have graduate degrees, but they employ field and laboratory technicians with bachelor's degrees.

Sources of Additional Information

For more information about the field of anthropology, contact:

American Anthropological Association
2200 Wilson Blvd., Ste. 600
Arlington, VA 22201
aaanet.org/careersbroch.htm

American Association of Museums
575 I St. NW, Ste. 400
Washington, DC 20005
aam-us.org

Archaeological Institute of America
656 Beacon St.
Boston, MA 02215
archaeological.org

Association of Science-Technology Centers
1025 Vermont Ave. NW, Ste. 500
Washington, DC 20005
astc.org

Canadian Sociology and Anthropology Association
1455, Boulevard de Maisonneuve Ouest
Montreal, QC 43G 1M8
alcor.concordia.ca/~csaa1

Peace Corps
1111 Twentieth St. NW
Washington, DC 20526
peacecorps.gov

Society for American Archaeology
900 Second St. NE, #12
Washington, DC 20002
saa.org

Society for Applied Anthropology
P.O. Box 2436
Oklahoma City, OK 73101
sfaa.net

The Smithsonian Institution Center for Education and Museum Studies has a website listing museum training programs offered by universities: museumstudies.si.edu/traindirect.htm.

3

SOCIOLOGY

SOCIOLOGY IS THE study of social life, social change, and the social causes and consequences of human behavior. Sociologists study groups, organizations, institutions, and societies to learn how social systems work.

Sociologists rely on the scientific method as the principal tool in explaining human relations. That is, they recognize a problem and, through observation and experimentation, collect data that enable them to form and test hypotheses. They use a range of research techniques, including survey research, and often work with very large statistical data sets.

Sociologists analyze the behavior of groups or social systems such as families and neighborhoods. Because sociology is the study of people in a social context, sociologists do not study individuals. Psychologists study individual behavior; sociologists are interested in collective behavior. Indeed, the term *sociology* comes from two Greek words that, taken together, mean "the study of groups." Sociologists focus on two areas: (1) the social relationships of those who belong to the group, and (2) the beliefs and values that are held by those in the group.

Groups are made up of individuals who have something in common. An example used by sociologists to show what is meant by a group involves people on an elevator. When they get on the elevator, they each have their own plans and purposes. If the elevator malfunctions, they join together and plan their exit. This collection of individuals becomes a group with a common goal.

Major Branches of Sociology

Humans form groups for many purposes. Each of these groups is a focus of study by sociologists.

Religious Groups

Religious denominations in the United States differ by race, social class, and age distribution, among other things. There has been an increase in the membership of evangelical and fundamentalist churches in recent years and a decline in the membership of mainline Protestant churches. In the sociology of religion these issues are studied.

Educational Systems

Another example of a group is the American educational system. Sociologists study educational systems to explore issues of inequality. They investigate the role of social class and family contributions to education. They study desegregation, school voucher plans, and school reform movements. Scientists who specialize in the sociology of education work on these issues.

Families

Another example of groups studied by sociologists is the family. The structure of families is not the same in all societies.

Many Chinese-Americans have extended families that include several generations in one household. In some extended families, all important decisions are made by the oldest man in the family. These are called patriarchal families. Families in some other societies are ruled by the oldest woman. Sociologists call them matriarchal families. Several Native American tribes were matriarchal societies.

Thirty years ago, the most common middle-class family pattern in the United States was the nuclear family, which was made up of a married man and woman who lived with their children. In the past several decades, this pattern has changed. Today many middle-class families are made up of single parents who live with their children. Family structures have been changed by death, separation, or divorce. Some unmarried women are raising children outside of marriage, and gay couples have adopted children. Sociologists study the individual roles of family members and their interactions. This work is done by scientists in the subfield of sociology of the family.

Sociologists Study Change

Sociologists study the effects of social change in all facets of life. For example, sociologists study the graying of America, the growing number of older people in our society. The study of the social problems faced by those growing older and the effect of the increasing number of dependent people on society is the focus of sociologists who specialize in gerontology.

Some of the other fields in which sociologists specialize are:

- **Social organization.** The study of the makeup and purpose of social groups.
- **Urban sociology.** The study of conditions in cities such as crime rates and housing patterns.
- **Criminology.** The study of crime, delinquency, crime prevention, and punishment.
- **Gender.** The study of changing sex roles.
- **Demography.** The study of the size, growth, characteristics, and movement of population.

Other subfields in sociology include the sociology of sports, the sociology of medicine, the sociology of work, the sociology of science, and the study of social problems such as addictions, suicide, and violence.

Sociologists study social issues that are found in the daily newspaper, such as the results of the Welfare to Work legislation, the decrease in public housing, and the changing distribution of ethnic groups in a community. Sociologists use the results of their research to help governments and other agencies formulate social policy.

Much of the research of sociologists is funded by the federal government or by foundations. Writing grant proposals to secure funding is an important part of a sociologist's job.

Careers in Sociology

Some sociologists are employed by government agencies, and through their work they deal with crime, poverty, public assistance programs, and racial relations. Sociologists in these areas are hired by the federal government to work in the Department of Health and Human Services, the Equal Employment Opportunity Commission, or in comparable jobs at the state level.

Sociologists specializing in demography work for the Bureau of the Census and international organizations such as the United Nations and the World Health Organization.

State and local governments employ sociologists who specialize in criminology. They work primarily for law enforcement agencies.

Some sociologists are self-employed. They often work in the areas of business, industry, and education as consultants. Sociologists who study the social factors that affect mental and public health are employed by health agencies and welfare organizations. Yet other sociologists are administrators. They manage social services programs and child welfare agencies.

In addition to these many different jobs, about eight thousand sociologists work in American colleges and universities, where they teach undergraduate and graduate students enrolled in sociology courses.

Related Careers

The following careers are some of those in which an understanding of sociology is valuable.

Social Work

Social workers are people who are specially trained to provide guidance and support to people in need. Social workers work with individuals, with groups, and with communities. Social workers must have as a minimum a bachelor's degree in social work. For many positions, a master's degree in social work is necessary. In all fifty states, social workers are licensed. To obtain a license, they must have a degree from an accredited school of social work, pass an examination, and work in a supervised setting. They must complete continuing education courses to renew their licenses.

The profession includes specialties such as psychiatric social work, school social work, hospital social work, industrial social work, child welfare work, and clinical social work. Social workers are parole officers and welfare caseworkers.

Through 2010, employment in social work is expected to grow faster than the average for other occupations. Average salaries for social workers range from $28,000 to $33,000.

Law Enforcement

Many police officers and law enforcement personnel have taken courses in sociology. Law enforcement officers are involved in community affairs. Frequently they meet with groups of citizens and try to increase the citizens' confidence in the police. Law enforcement officers also teach community groups how to help fight crime.

Human Services Workers

Today there are many paraprofessional jobs in human services agencies. They involve working in group homes and halfway houses. Community mental health centers and substance abuse programs also employ human services workers. Some are community outreach workers and others are social work assistants. All human services workers are under the direction of professional staff members.

Job duties of human services workers vary, depending on the people receiving services. Human services workers in health-care settings lead groups, organize activities, and counsel clients. Others who work in social services agencies interview clients and determine how the agency can help them. Many human services workers maintain records and files. Case aides assist clients in many ways. They accompany them to adult day-care programs or doctors' offices.

Some work in public housing projects, where they help the tenants by providing information about regulations and services. Human services workers are employed in group homes. There they help adults who need supervision or assistance on a daily basis.

Recreation Workers

Recreation workers plan activities that help others enjoy their leisure time. They are employed by health clubs, theme parks, campgrounds, and senior centers. Others are hired by adult day-care programs, nursing homes, and correctional institutions. Many recreation workers are employed by organizations such as the Girl Scouts and Red Cross. A large number of recreation workers are part-time employees. Some part-time, seasonal jobs include playground leaders and camp counselors.

Employment Opportunities

About 80 percent of sociologists with Ph.D.s are employed by colleges and universities. The U.S. Department of Labor predicts strong competition for people seeking positions at any level. Sociologists trained in research methods, advanced statistics, and the use of computers will have the widest choice of jobs. Demand is expected to be strong for research personnel in the areas of rural sociology, community development, population analysis, public opinion research, medical sociology, juvenile delinquency, and evaluation research.

Students who major in gerontology are expected to find a growing number of career opportunities through the next decade. In addition to gerontology, other areas of demand will be demography and criminology. Sociologists will also be needed to administer and evaluate programs intended to cope with social and welfare problems.

It is expected that the number of those graduating with advanced degrees in sociology will be greater than the number of available jobs. Those with doctorates in sociology will face keen competition for faculty positions. An increasing number of those with Ph.D.s in sociology will be employed by government agencies and research organizations. Those skilled in research methods, including survey techniques, statistics, and computer science, will have the most job opportunities.

Those with master's degrees will face competition for positions in research firms, business, and government. Graduates with bachelor's degrees in sociology will find some entry-level positions in business, industry, and government.

Salaries and Earnings

According to the Bureau of Labor Statistics, the average salary for sociologists is $56,560. Sociologists employed by educational institutions earn an average of about $57,500 a year. The average beginning salary for an assistant professor is $42,800.

In recent years, the average entry-level salary in the federal government for sociologists with a bachelor's degree ranged from

$21,900 to $27,200. The starting salary in the federal government for those with a master's degree was about $33,300 a year, and with a Ph.D. it was $40,200.

Preparing for a Career in Sociology

To prepare to study sociology in college, you should take high school courses in English, mathematics, and the social, biological, and physical sciences. You will also find it helpful to learn as much as possible about computers.

Working with people in groups is also an excellent preparation. For example, if you are interested in a career in gerontology, you might work as a volunteer in a nursing home or senior citizens center. Other job opportunities that will help you are assisting in playground activities or youth programs.

Educational Requirements

A bachelor's degree is essential for any entry-level position, and a master's degree is recommended, or in many instances, required. A Ph.D. is necessary for positions in most colleges and universities. The doctorate is also required to work as research project directors, in administrative positions, or as consultants. It is expected that as the job market tightens through the next decade, a Ph.D. will be required for all professional and academic positions in sociology.

Sociologists with master's degrees are employed in administrative and research positions by private industries and public agencies. Those who have earned a bachelor's degree in sociology find jobs in related fields. Some work as counselors or recreation directors in public and private agencies. Others who hold a bachelor's degree are hired as interviewers by social services agencies. Those who meet state requirements for teacher certification may become sociology teachers in secondary schools.

A degree in sociology provides an excellent preparation for those planning careers in law, journalism, and social work.

For many paraprofessional positions, an associate degree in sociology is desired. Included are such career options as recreation workers and human services workers.

Sources of Additional Information

For more information about careers in sociology, contact:

American Society of Criminology
1314 Kinnear Rd., Ste. 212
Columbus, OH 43212
asc41.com

American Sociological Association
1307 New York Ave. NW, Ste. 700
Washington, DC 20005
asanet.org

A brochure, "Careers in Sociology," is available on its website at asanet .org/student/career/homepage.html. Also, single copies of "Majoring in Sociology: A Guide for Students," a publication designed for high school and undergraduate students, are available free from the ASA executive office. Multiple copies are twenty-five cents each.

Canadian Sociology and Anthropology Association
1455, Boulevard de Maisonneuve Ouest
Montreal, QC H3G 1M8
alcor.concordia.ca/~csaa1

Gerontological Society
1030 Fifteenth St. NW, Ste. 250
Washington, DC 20005
geron.org

Humanities and Social Sciences Federation of Canada
151 Slater St., #415
Ottawa, ON K1P 5H3
fedcan.ca

Population Association of America
8630 Fenton St., Ste. 640
Silver Spring, MD 20910
popassoc.org

Population Reference Bureau
1875 Connecticut Ave. NW, Ste. 520
Washington, DC 20009
prb.org

Sociological Practice Association
P.O. Box 15
Wyncote, PA 19095
socpractice.org

Additional information about careers in selected allied fields is available from:

American Association for Leisure and Recreation
1900 Association Dr.
Reston, VA 20191
aahperd.org/aalr/template.cfm

American Camping Association
Bradford Woods
5000 State Road 67 N
Martinsville, IN 46151
acacamps.org

Canadian Association of Schools of Social Work
1398 Star Top Rd.
Ottawa, ON K1B 4V7
cassw-access.ca

Employee Services and Management Association
2211 York Rd., Ste. 207
Oak Brook, IL 60523
esmassu.org

National Association of Social Workers
750 First St. NE, Ste. 700
Washington, DC 20002
naswdc.org

National Organization for Human Service Education
9001 Braddock Rd., Ste. 380
Springfield, VA 22151
nohse.org

4

PSYCHOLOGY

HAVE YOU EVER wondered why people behave or act as they do? Psychology is the social science that studies the human mind and human behavior. Indeed, the word *psychology* is derived from two Greek words that, taken together, mean "the study of the mind."

The mind is that part of human beings that thinks, feels, chooses, decides, and perceives. Thus psychology, the study of the mind, focuses on thought processes, emotions, and behavior.

Psychologists investigate a person's ability to learn and the effect of emotions on human health and behavior. Psychologists use their skills and training to counsel or advise individuals and groups.

Psychologists make up the largest occupation in the social sciences. More than 182,000 people work in the field of psychology. Most of them are employed in the areas of research and counseling. More than 40 percent are self-employed. Yet psychology is a relatively new science as compared to history or geography. It is only about a century old.

If you choose a career in psychology, a bachelor's degree with a major in psychology is usually not enough to qualify for a job in the field. A position as a psychologist generally requires a doctoral degree.

Major Branches of Psychology

The field of psychology should not be confused with psychiatry. Psychiatrists are medical doctors. Though the work of psychologists and psychiatrists sometimes is similar, psychiatrists are able to prescribe medication while psychologists are not. The following are the major branches of the field of psychology.

Experimental Psychologists

Experimental psychologists make up the largest group in psychological research. Experimental psychologists are researchers who study perception, sensation, and learning. They also study the anatomy of the brain and neural networks. They study human beings and sometimes use animals such as mice, rats, and monkeys in experiments. The work of experimental psychologists is similar in many ways to that of biologists, and much of their course work is in the natural sciences. They design and conduct research in laboratories on college campuses and in large industries. Some experimental psychologists are involved in research for the government.

Experimental psychologists use observation and measurement techniques. Because they conduct experiments, they must know statistics. Advanced courses in probability (which is used to predict results) and inferential statistics are required as part of the training of experimental psychologists. Because experimental psychologists process much information, they use computers in their work.

Though they may work in private industry or in laboratories, most experimental psychologists teach in colleges and universities.

Industrial or Organizational Psychologists

Industrial psychologists apply psychological principles to human behavior in the workplace. They are concerned with such aspects of work as job satisfaction, efficiency, and employee training programs. People working in this field investigate working conditions and the relationships that exist between employers and employees. Industrial psychologists examine the work environment and develop plans for changing an organization's structure to increase employee satisfaction and thus improve productivity.

Industrial psychologists apply psychological techniques to personnel administration, management, and marketing. They screen job applicants and take part in employee training and development. They are employed in business, industry, and government. They often work as consultants, brought in by management to solve a particular problem.

Clinical Psychologists

Clinical psychologists diagnose and treat psychological disorders. They work with the mentally or emotionally ill. They administer psychological tests and work directly with patients to find the causes of their problems. Interpretation of these tests, along with interviews and observation, help the psychologist make a diagnosis. Clinical psychologists use psychotherapy as a treatment method. The field of clinical psychology and its methods overlap with psychiatry. Clinical psychologists may refer patients to psychiatrists if they think the patients could benefit from treatment with drugs.

PUBLIC LIBRARY
DANVILLE, ILLINOIS

Like psychiatrists, clinical psychologists must usually complete an internship during their training.

Hospitals and clinics, schools, and prisons employ some clinical psychologists. Other clinical psychologists have private practices where they treat clients. They may work with individuals or families or provide group psychotherapy. They may also administer community or state mental health programs.

Some clinical psychologists teach at the university level, training graduate students studying for careers in clinical psychology.

Developmental Psychologists

Developmental psychologists trace the stages of human growth from birth to death. They study the patterns and causes of changes in people's behavior as they pass through life. Developmental psychologists realize that people think, perceive, and behave differently during different periods of their lifetimes.

Some developmental psychologists specialize in human behavior during infancy, childhood, and adolescence. Others study the many changes that take place as people mature and age. Although this field has generally concentrated on children, in recent years there has been increasing interest in the issues of maturity and old age. Developmental psychologists know the sequence of normal human development and the difficulties that result if this development is not normal.

Developmental psychologists tend to teach in colleges and universities, often in colleges of education, but they may also work in research institutes concerned with child welfare or gerontology.

Educational Psychologists

Educational psychologists study the learning process. They investigate intellectual growth. Educational psychologists use their knowledge of child development to help schools plan curricula and activities that are appropriate for pupils' levels of development. Educational psychologists analyze the educational needs of their clients. They develop instructional materials and assess their effectiveness.

Educational psychologists are employed by boards of education and also work in business and industry. Some are hired by the armed services to evaluate their instructional programs. Many teach in colleges and universities.

Social Psychologists

Social psychologists study how individuals perceive and interact with others. They frequently work with groups, studying group behaviors and attitudes.

They examine people's interactions with others, focusing on their social environment. Some of the areas of specialization for social psychologists are group behavior, leadership, and group attitudes. This is an applied area of psychology, and practitioners often work in organizational development or marketing research in corporations.

Social psychology is often a research specialty in universities. Social psychologists engaged in research are interested in group behavior, attitudes, and perception.

Counseling Psychologists

Counseling psychologists help people with the daily problems of life. Each year about thirty-four million Americans seek the help of counseling psychologists. Not surprisingly, counseling psychology is the area in the discipline that is most familiar to Americans.

Counseling psychologists are trained in testing procedures. They also interview and counsel clients. Counseling psychologists often work with normal or moderately maladjusted persons in Veterans'

Administration hospitals, mental health centers, university counseling centers, or rehabilitation facilities. The largest number of counseling psychologists is in private practice. These psychologists have their own offices, often in a group practice with other psychologists. They use many techniques to advise people on how to deal with the problems of everyday life. Counseling psychologists are concerned with their clients' personal, social, educational, and vocational lives.

School Psychologists

School psychologists work in elementary and secondary schools. They help pupils who have problems of behavior and achievement both individually and in groups. They also test pupils who seem to have learning problems. School psychologists develop individualized programs for pupils with learning disabilities. They consult with teachers and parents about the developmental needs of individual students. They work with pupils, their parents, and teachers to resolve behavior problems. They may be responsible for running drug and alcohol abuse programs.

Some school psychologists are also psychometrists. They administer and interpret standardized examinations such as intelligence tests and personality surveys.

School psychology is closely related to the fields of educational and developmental psychology. It is a graduate specialty in many master's and doctoral degree programs.

Related Careers

There are many career opportunities in fields related to psychology. There are several fields of specialization in counseling that usually require only a bachelor's degree or less.

Rehabilitation counselors help those with disabilities become more self-sufficient. They evaluate their clients' individual potential for employment. Many rehabilitation counselors work in health facilities, Department of Veterans Affairs hospitals, and substance abuse clinics.

Employment counselors help their clients explore and evaluate their education, training, and skills to find suitable employment. They may arrange for them to take aptitude and achievement tests. They help clients find jobs and complete the application forms needed in new positions. Employment counselors are employed by nonprofit organizations such as Goodwill and by social agencies such as community centers. Counselors employed by colleges and vocational schools help students find employment.

Mental health counselors help individuals and families deal with family conflicts, substance abuse, and problems at work. Some mental health counselors help rape victims. Many counsel families coping with illness and death. Mental health counselors cooperate with other professionals such as psychiatrists, social workers, and psychologists.

Courses in psychology are also valuable for those who select careers in teaching, social work, and religion. Protestant ministers, Catholic priests, and Jewish rabbis counsel members of their faith. They advise individuals seeking guidance, do marriage counseling, and console the bereaved. Because they frequently work with groups, training in social psychology is beneficial.

Employment Opportunities

The prospects for teachers and researchers in the field of psychology in four-year colleges or universities are presently limited, though they may improve as faculty members retire over the next decade. Some two-year colleges are adding faculty.

Positions in psychological research depend on funding to support research programs. Federal and state funding are not expected to increase significantly. Some private foundations support research programs to investigate human behavior.

The current growth in regional and local mental health facilities will open more employment opportunities. The increase in services provided for senior citizens indicates a need for more professionals trained in psychology to work with older people.

Employment opportunities are excellent in fields such as counseling psychology, industrial psychology, and clinical psychology.

Salaries and Earnings

According to the National Association of Colleges and Employers Salary Survey, the average beginning salary for someone with a bachelor's degree in psychology is $26,000. However, most of those graduates took jobs in business, human services, or other fields. According to an American Psychological Association salary survey of psychologists with a doctorate, counseling psychologists have an average salary of $66,500, clinical psychologists have an average salary of $72,000, and school psychologists earn an average salary of $77,000. Psychologists in private practice typically have the highest incomes. According to the Bureau of Labor Statistics, the average salary for industrial/organizational psychologists is $70,000.

The salaries for psychologists who teach in colleges and universities average $55,000 a year. Many psychologists earn additional money through consulting or as members of a group practice.

Preparing for a Career in Psychology

Probably the most important high school preparation for a major in psychology is a firm foundation in mathematics and English composition. An ability to use computers is essential in the field of psychology. If you can, take a course in computers and their use while in high school.

If your high school offers a course in psychology, you would be wise to take it. It will introduce you to many of the topics you will study if you major or minor in psychology in college.

Educational Requirements

All of the professional positions in psychology require a minimum of a bachelor's degree in psychology from a college or university. Most professional positions in the field require additional study beyond the undergraduate degree.

However, some state or community agencies offer a limited number of positions for graduates with bachelor's degrees in psychology. In addition, many psychology majors obtain positions in business and industry.

Recently there has been an increase in the paraprofessional career opportunities in some fields of psychology, such as mental health assistant. Mental health assistants are paraprofessionals in a facility such as a mental health center or senior citizen service center. Their duties include screening new clients, contacting patients, and keeping records. For this position, an associate degree in psychology is usually sufficient.

Certification

In most states, psychologists who offer any type of patient care (including clinical, counseling, and school psychologists) must be licensed to practice. Licenses are issued by state agencies with names such as Office of the Professions, Department of Professional Regulation, or State Psychology Board. A publication of the Association of State and Provincial Psychology Boards, *Handbook of*

Licensure and Certification, lists certification requirements and agencies for U.S. states and Canadian provinces. It is available online at asppb.org/pubs/handbookusr.asp.

Generally, to be certified in psychology requires a doctorate (although some states will allow those with master's degrees in psychology to practice in a supervised setting), the passing of a national examination called the Examination for Professional Practice in Psychology, and supervised experience or an internship. Psychologists usually must obtain continuing education credits to renew their licenses.

Voluntary Certification

In addition, practitioners in clinical, counseling, and industrial psychology can apply to be board-certified by the American Board of Professional Psychology. The American Board of Examiners in Professional Psychology issues diplomas to applicants who hold a doctorate in psychology and have experience in their specialty. In addition, they must pass written, oral, and practical exams in the general field of psychology and in their specialty. Psychologists who attain this certification are called diplomates.

Sources of Additional Information

For more information about careers in psychology, contact:

American Board of Professional Psychology
514 E. Capitol Ave.
Jefferson City, MO 65101
abpp.org

American Counseling Association
5999 Stevenson Ave.
Alexandria, VA 22304
counseling.org

American Psychological Association
Educational Directorate
750 First St. NW
Washington, DC 20002

The APA has a brochure, "Careers in Psychology in the 21st Century," on its website at apa.org/students/brochure/index.html.

American Psychological Society
1010 Vermont Ave. NW, Ste. 1100
Washington, DC 20005
psychologicalscience.org

American School Counselor Association
801 N. Fairfax St., Ste. 310
Alexandria, VA 22314
schoolcounselor.org

Association of State and Provincial Psychology Boards
P.O. Box 241245
Montgomery, AL 36124
asppb.org

Canadian Psychological Association
151 Slater St., Ste. 205
Ottawa, ON K1P 5H3
cpa.ca

Commission on Rehabilitation Counselor Certification
1835 Rohlwing Rd., Ste. E
Rolling Meadows, IL 60008
crccertification.com

Council on Rehabilitation Education
1835 Rohlwing Rd., Ste. E
Rolling Meadows, IL 60008
core-rehab.org

National Association of School Psychologists
4340 East West Highway, Ste. 402
Bethesda, MD 20814
nasponline.org

National Board for Certified Counselors
5999 Stevenson Ave.
Alexandria, VA 22304
nbcc.org

National Council on Rehabilitation Education
Rehabilitation Counseling Program
Kremen School of Education
California State University, Fresno
5005 N. Maple Ave., M/S ED3
Fresno, CA 90740
rehabeducators.org

National Mental Health Association
2001 N. Beauregard St., 12th Fl.
Arlington, VA 22311
nmha.org

National Rehabilitation Counseling Association
8807 Sudley Rd., Ste. 102
Manassas, VA 22110
nrca-net.org

Rehabilitation Services Administration
U.S. Department of Education
400 Maryland Ave. SW, Rm. 3329-MES
Washington, DC 20202
ed.gov/offices/osers/rsa/index.html

For more information about careers in religious service, contact:

American Association for Pastoral Counselors
9504A Lee Highway
Fairfax, VA 22031
aapc.org

Hebrew Union College
Jewish Institute of Religion
3101 Clifton Ave.
Cincinnati, OH 45220
huc.edu
(Reform)

Jewish Theological Seminary of America
3080 Broadway
New York, NY 10027
jtsa.edu
(Conservative)

The Rabbi Isaac Elchanan Theological Seminary
Yeshiva University
2540 Amsterdam Ave.
New York, NY 10033
riets.edu
(Orthodox)

Reconstructionist Rabbinical College
1299 Church Rd.
Wyncote, PA 19095
rrc.edu

Serra International
65 E. Wacker Pl., Ste. 802
Chicago, IL 60603
serraus.org

5

HISTORY

HISTORY IS ONE of the oldest social sciences. Even those who lived in ancient times studied it. Greek and Roman historians wrote books that are still read today. The word *history* is derived from a Latin word meaning "narrative" or "story." Historians study the past experiences of humankind as they were preserved in written records. They then tell the story of human events and provide an interpretation of those events. We study history to help us learn from the past, so we can better understand the present and plan for the future.

History is a hybrid of the humanities and the social sciences. Historians use some of the same techniques that humanists such as art historians or literary historians use, and like them, historians are interested in values. However, history in the twentieth century has moved from being simply a narration of events to using many of the social sciences' approaches to research. For example, a historian studying Hitler might use some of the techniques of a psychologist. A historian looking at slavery might use statistical techniques. But while most social scientists are able to make direct observations of what they are studying, historians only have written records of the past to go by.

If you want to understand why events happened the way they did, you have a good reason to study history. If you enjoy stories about the choices people made and the events that resulted from their choices or if you like to solve mysteries about people, places, and events, you should consider studying history. Learning about the past can give you insight into the motivating forces of human life: love and hate, oppression and reform, hope and despair, wealth and poverty. The study of history can prepare you for everyday life by helping you to understand how people tried to solve their problems in the past. As twentieth-century French writer and art historian André Malraux observed, "Our heritage is composed of all the voices that can answer our questions."

Major Branches of History

Because history is concerned about the past of the world's peoples, its scope is tremendous. There is so much to study in history that its subject matter is divided in several ways:

Time Period

Its first division is based on time, or when the people being studied lived. Historians divide history into three periods: ancient, medieval, and modern.

Ancient history includes the time when the written records of the past were first kept through the earliest centuries after the birth of Christ. Some of the people studied in ancient history are the Greeks, Romans, Chinese, and Egyptians.

The second time period is the medieval, or the Middle Ages. It includes events that took place several centuries after the birth of Christ until the seventeenth century. Some of the subjects studied during this period are the Crusades, explorers such as Christopher Columbus and Marco Polo, and the Byzantine Empire.

Modern times make up the third division. Included in a study of modern history are the peoples who lived from the Renaissance or about 1600 to the present. Some of the events that took place during this period are the rise of the Ottoman Empire, the founding of the American nation, and World War II.

Geography or Place

The subject matter of history can also be divided by geography, in other words, by nation or region. Some examples are American history, Pennsylvania history, European history, and Asian studies.

Topics

Finally, the subject matter of history can be divided by topics. Included in this division are the Industrial Revolution and the Age of Enlightenment, for example.

Areas of Specialization

There are four major areas of specialization in history.

Political history is the study of how people through the ages have been led and governed. Included in a study of political history are wars, revolutions, governments, laws, and treaties.

Social history examines the common people in history. Some topics included in social history are immigration, industrialization, and urbanization. This is sometimes described as "history from the bottom up" because it emphasizes the study of average people rather than that of kings and presidents, which fall into the domain of political history.

Economic history investigates how people through the ages have provided for their wants and needs and how economies have been organized. Some topics included in economic history are the plantation system and labor organizations.

Cultural history focuses on the values, beliefs, and goals of people who lived in the past. Included in a study of cultural history are topics such as Marxist communism and the Catholic Church in the Middle Ages.

Biography is a form of historical writing. Historians provide a picture of an era by writing a biography of an important person from that period.

Careers in History

A range of exciting careers exists in the field of history for those with varied interests. Whether you excel at researching, writing, or lecturing, there's sure to be some career path that will suit your talents and interests. The following describes a few of the possible career paths for history buffs.

Professional Historians

Professional historians describe and analyze the events of the past through research and writing. Historians specialize in one or more branches of history. Scholars may describe themselves as colonial American historians or as medieval French historians or as historians of modern Latin America.

In addition to specializing in a period and part of the world, historians have an unlimited number of topics on which to concentrate. Some historians study sports history, the history of the environment, women's history, the history of education, or the history of science. Other fields they might choose include oral history, popular culture, or ethnic history.

Oral history involves speaking with those who have lived during a specific time and recording conversations with them. Interviewing a soldier who fought in Vietnam is an example of oral history.

Popular culture is concerned with people's values, activities, and preferences. Analyzing how John Wayne's films shaped modern culture's perceptions of the Old West is an example of an activity in which a historian who specializes in popular culture might be involved.

Ethnic history is another specialty of some historians. Investigating the influence of Americans of Bohemian descent in Cleveland, Ohio, or the lives of African-Americans in nineteenth century Philadelphia are examples of ethnic studies.

Professional historians prepare in narrative or outline form a chronological record of past and current events dealing with a specific phase of human activity. They gather historical data from indexes, catalogs, archives, court records, news files, diaries, and other published and unpublished materials. Professional historians emphasize the use of primary sources, documents that date from the period being studied. They evaluate these sources on the basis of authenticity and reliability.

Colleges and universities employ most professional historians. There they teach undergraduate students enrolled in history survey classes, and they also teach in their area of specialization. They instruct graduate students and advise them as they complete their advanced studies.

Public Historians

This title describes historians who do research but are not employed by universities. They may work for a government agency such as the National Park Service or the army, for historical societies and museums, or they may make a living by publishing their books. The educated public enjoys books by historians—sometimes these books become bestsellers. Writers like Bruce Catton and Barbara Tuchman wrote enormously successful histories.

Public historians also can engage in historical research for individuals, institutions, and organizations. They can be hired to write a company history, for example.

Archivists

Archivists evaluate and edit permanent records and historical documents. They also ensure the safekeeping of archival documents. Archivists must be knowledgeable about the conservation of paper documents. They frequently must establish the date of a document's origin to determine its historical value. They prepare document descriptions and other reference materials.

Archivists decide what parts of the information produced by the government, schools and colleges, corporations, and other organizations should be kept and made part of the historical record. Frequently they decide which items of their archival collection should be exhibited. Their collections may include coins, stamps, photographs, documents, clothing, maps, and historic sites, as well as paper records.

Archivists also classify the information in their collections so it can be easily located. They decide whether it should be stored in its original form or if it should be stored on microfilm or as computer records.

Archivists are employed by museums, religious denominations, associations, historical societies, and corporate, university, or independent research libraries. There they assemble, analyze, preserve, and index documentary material for scholarly use.

Historical Consultants

Historical consultants assist editors, publishers, filmmakers, and television producers of historically oriented materials. When you next view a historical film or documentary, read the credits. Frequently you will find the name of a historian who helped in its production. Although this not a full-time job, it enables the historian to disseminate his or her work to the wider public.

Related Careers

History majors often enter law school or business school. They are also employed in fields including labor, industry, communication, and government civil service.

Students who combine history with strong backgrounds in other subjects may work in such careers as journalism and public service. Businesses are interested in hiring people with the broad educational background that history majors have.

Persons with historical training are especially well suited for work in government careers. History students have a real advantage when taking the various civil service examinations. History graduates can find jobs in diplomatic and welfare services and governmental research and record keeping at the local, state, and national levels.

For employment in fields allied to history, training in a foreign language is desirable. In some, such as the Foreign Service, it is mandatory.

Employment Opportunities

Opportunities for employment rest largely with an individual's training and determination. The employment potential in the field of history in colleges and universities is limited. According to the American Historical Association, more than a third of all history departments reported hiring new assistant professors in 2001, but this accounted for only about one-third of all Ph.D.s awarded in history that year.

The best prospects for archivists are with government agencies. Large corporations employ some archivists to maintain corporate records that explain the company's history.

Salaries and Earnings

According to the National Association of Colleges and Employers Salary Survey, the national average starting salary for a college graduate with a bachelor's degree in history in 2002 was $30,000. Archivists generally earn an average of $28,000 the first year of employment.

The average starting salary for historians employed by government is $40,000. According to the Bureau of Labor Statistics, the average historian makes $44,850.

According to the American Historical Association, the average beginning salary for an assistant professor with a Ph.D. in 2001–2002 was about $40,000. Most professional historians supplement their regular salaries by consulting, lecturing, and writing.

Preparing for a Career in History

Taking as many courses in history as possible, including advanced placement courses, will be useful for the future historian. Being able to write well is important for historians, so take as much English as possible as well as other courses that require research and writing. Increasingly, historians use computers in their research, so a working knowledge of computers is necessary. Studying a foreign language is also useful. Volunteer work in a historical society or museum will be good experience.

Educational Requirements

Advanced education and the acquisition of research skills are key factors in promotion in the field of history. A Ph.D. is a minimum requirement for history faculty in four-year colleges and universities. Positions as archivists usually require a master's degree in history or library science; an increasing number of archivists have double master's degrees in history and library science. A doctorate in history or a related field may be needed for some advanced positions in archives. Teaching history at the middle or high school level requires a bachelor's degree and certification by the state.

Sources of Additional Information

For more information about careers in history, contact:

American Association for State and Local History
1717 Church St.
Nashville, TN 37203
aaslh.org

American Historical Association
400 A St. SE
Washington, DC 20003
theaha.org

The association has two useful articles on its website: "Careers in History," theaha.org/careers/index.html, and "Why Become a Historian," theaha.org/pubs/why/blackeyintro.htm.

American Institute for Conservation of Historic and Artistic Works
1717 K St. NW, Ste. 200
Washington, DC 20006
aic.stanford.edu

Canadian Council of Archives
West Memorial Bldg., #1109
344 Wellington St.
Ottawa, ON K1A 0N3
cdncouncilarchives.ca

Canadian Historical Association
395 Wellington St.
Ottawa, ON K1A 0N3
cha-shc.ca

Center for Education and Museum Programs
The Smithsonian Institution
P.O. Box 37012, A&I 1163, MRC 402
Washington, DC 20013
smithsonianeducation.org

National Trust for Historic Preservation
1785 Massachusetts Ave. NW
Washington, DC 20036
nthp.org

Organization of American Historians
112 North Bryan St.
Bloomington, IN 47408
oah.org

Society of American Archivists
527 S. Wells St., 5th Fl.
Chicago, IL 60607
archivists.org

6

GEOGRAPHY

GEOGRAPHERS STUDY THE distribution of places on the face of the earth and the relationship between people and these places.

Geography is one of the oldest academic disciplines. Writers in ancient Greece described their physical surroundings and recorded their distant travels. The word *geography* is derived from two Greek words: one means earth and the other means writings or description. This term is an apt one for a science that studies landforms such as mountains, plains, and valleys. But geography is a social science. This means that geographers also study the various interrelationships between humans and their environments.

Geography is not just the study of where, how long, how far, and how big. It is the study of the earth's surface and the way that different environments affect the people who live there, as well as how people affect the places where they live. Geographers were among the first to point out that changes to the environment caused by humans are threatening the balance of life. Geographers are active in the study of global warming, desertification, deforestation, and pollution.

Major Branches of Geography

Generally, geography is divided into two areas: physical geography and human geography.

Physical geographers study topics such as landforms and the distribution of plants and animals. Usually physical geography is not regarded as a social science. It is considered one of the physical sciences, overlapping fields such as geology and biology.

Human geography, which includes areas of study such as cultural geography, urban geography, ecological geography, and political geography, is regarded as a social science. In each of these areas of study, humans are an important part of the geographer's work.

For example, human geography explains why high school basketball is such a phenomenon in the state of Indiana. So enthused are its fans during the tournaments that lead to the state championship that the period is described as Hoosier hysteria. The reasons for Indiana's fascination with high school basketball lie in the state's history, economics, and, particularly, its geography.

About one hundred years ago, Indiana was primarily an agricultural state. The farmers who lived there worked very long hours. Their busiest seasons were spring, when they planted their crops; summer, when they tended them; and fall, when they harvested them. During the winter, farmers had fewer responsibilities. During these winter months, their children also had more leisure time. They attended small, rural schools that did not have much money for recreational equipment.

Each of these factors is important. Basketball is an indoor sport, so it can be played throughout the winter. It requires far fewer players than sports such as football. It requires little equipment other than a ball and hoop. A player's shooting skills can be developed by individual practice, with no other players involved.

All of these factors caused basketball to take a firm hold on Indiana's people. The tradition of a century continues today, so that Indiana's enthusiasm for the sport is known around the world.

This human approach to geography can make study in the field fascinating. Perhaps more important, knowledge of geography will help the people of today understand and care for their world.

Careers in Geography

As with the other branches of the social sciences we've discussed thus far, the possible career paths for those interested in the field of geography are many and varied. More and more often, technology plays a key role in the advancement of the work of those engaged in geography, so this field might be a particularly good choice for those who are interested in computers and new applications for their use. The following are a few of the exciting possibilities for those interested in working in this field.

Cartographers

Cartographers make maps. Some of the maps they make include physical maps that show continents, oceans, and features such as mountains and rivers. Political maps show boundaries of states, provinces, and countries. Another kind of map is a population density map, which shows how many people live in a specific area.

Others who are involved in cartography are organizers, researchers, graphic artists, and photographers. Cartographers are frequently employed by the government and in industry.

The development of geographic information systems (GIS) has revolutionized the work of cartographers and other geographers. New computer systems have been created for the capture, updating, manipulation, and display of geographic information. Sometimes images of earth are captured by remote satellites and fed into computers, providing far more accurate maps of our world. This is called remote sensing. Knowledge of computers and GIS is now essential for anyone working in the field.

Urban and Regional Planners

Urban and regional planners develop plans for the orderly growth of communities. They must have training in geography in addition to planning. They are concerned with efficient land use for residential, business, and community purposes.

Urban and regional planners are concerned with things such as the location of schools, streets and highways, water lines, and recreational sites. Urban and regional planners can specialize in areas such as physical design, public transportation, and community relations. Many urban and regional planners are concerned with the renovation of run-down districts. They are also concerned with the reconstruction and preservation of historic buildings.

Some urban and regional planners are employed by city and state planning departments. Others are employed by community development agencies. Urban and regional planners also work for architectural and surveying firms and large land developers.

In 2003, urban and regional planners held about thirty-five thousand jobs. According to the Department of Labor, local government planning agencies such as cities and counties employed more than 60 percent of them.

College Teaching

Some geographers teach undergraduates who are studying geography in universities and colleges. Others train graduate students for careers as professional geographers and researchers.

Geographers in Government

Geographers in government and industry are usually not called by that name. They frequently have titles such as intelligence officer, transportation coordinator, political analyst, and planning director. The Central Intelligence Agency, the National Imaging and Mapping Agency, and the Department of the Interior employ most of the geographers in the federal government.

Related Careers

Many careers are allied with the field of geography. Some of the job titles are map librarian, aerial photo interpreter, real estate consultant, and meteorologist.

Map librarians build map collections in large academic, public, and some special libraries. Since most maps are published by government agencies, map librarians must be familiar with government publications. Librarians acquire, catalog, and classify maps and help researchers use them. Map librarians also must have an understanding of geographic information systems and know how to help users both find electronic maps and data and manipulate them.

Employment Opportunities

About 25 percent of all professional geographers find employment in local, state, or federal government; the armed services; or international organizations.

The greatest demand for geographers is in geographic information systems and other areas of technical data interpretation, remote sensing, cartography, planning, market research, and site analysis.

Employment for planning professionals is expected to grow more slowly than the average for all occupations. People who specialize have better opportunities, and much new growth is occurring in private consulting firms rather than with government agencies.

Due to the large number of retirements in academic libraries, opportunities for map librarians may be better than average.

Salaries and Earnings

According to the Bureau of Labor Statistics, the average salary for a geographer is $50,130. Cartographers with the U.S. Census Bureau earn beginning salaries of $32,000 with a bachelor's degree, $40,000 with a master's degree, and $48,000 with a doctoral degree. A beginning instructor of geography at a four-year college earns about $37,700 for the academic year.

According to the Bureau of Labor Statistics, the average salary of an urban planner is $50,430. State agencies pay urban and regional planners more than city, county, or regional governments. The average annual salary paid by states is $45,000. Salaries of planners in large areas may be as much as $10,000 a year higher than those of planners in smaller ones. Salaries of urban and regional planners employed by the federal government range from $32,000 to $87,000.

Beginning salaries for academic librarians average $32,000. The average salary for librarians in college and university libraries is $43,000. Government librarians earn on average $63,600.

Preparing for a Career in Geography

If you are preparing for a career in geography, several courses in high school will help you. A solid foundation in communication skills is essential. If your high school offers courses in world or human geography, it would be beneficial to take them. A course in computer science would be extremely useful.

Educational Requirements

An undergraduate degree in geography is necessary for most entry-level positions in geography. However, a four-year degree may not be essential for some beginning positions in the field of cartography.

Four-year colleges and universities require a doctoral degree for positions in teaching and research. A master's degree is required for teaching in two-year colleges and technical schools.

Urban planners need a master's degree in planning. Map librarians have a master's degree in library science.

Sources of Additional Information

For more information about careers in the field of geography, contact:

American Congress on Surveying and Mapping
6 Montgomery Village Ave., Ste. 403
Gaithersburg, MD 20879
acsm.net

Association of American Geographers
1710 Sixteenth St. NW
Washington, DC 20009
aag.org/careers/intro.html

Canadian Association of Geographers
Burnside Hall, McGill University
805 Rue Sherbrooke Ouest
Montreal, QC H3A 2K6
cag.uwindsor.ca

Information on careers in urban and regional planning is available from:

American Planning Association
1776 Massachusetts Ave. NW
Washington, DC 20036
planning.org/careers

Association of Collegiate Schools of Planning
6311 Mallard Trace
Tallahassee, FL 32312
acsp.org

For more information on careers in map librarianship, contact:

Map and Geography Round Table
American Library Association
50 E. Huron St.
Chicago, IL 60611
magert.whoi.edu:8000

7

Political Science

POLITICAL SCIENCE IS the study of the origin and development of political systems and the political process. Political scientists study all aspects of political behavior, such as the interrelationships of political institutions. They focus on how governments make decisions and investigate the content, implementation, and effects of those decisions. They study public opinion and ideology. They conduct research and analyze and interpret the results of their studies. They prepare reports that detail their findings and make recommendations for public policy.

The world and its problems are both the main concern and the principal laboratory of the modern political scientist. Political scientists study the political behavior of people, groups, and nations in an effort to understand why they behave as they do, to predict what they will do next, and sometimes to suggest how they should act in the future.

Major Branches of Political Science

There are no generally agreed upon subfields in political science. The oldest field in the discipline is the study of government.

Political scientists study government and its institutions, including city councils, state legislatures, national assemblies, and political parties. Political scientists research pressure groups like lobbyists and government branches such as the judiciary. They investigate the ways in which people organize, distribute, and use political power. The scope of study can range from international organizations such as the European Union to meetings of the local school board.

Political scientists study political theory, which includes ideologies like communism or other belief systems. They investigate the nature of power and the psychology of leadership.

Political scientists study comparative politics, looking at the way other cultures organize their political systems and the relationships between nations. They use computer models to do some of this research.

Political scientists also study public law, which deals with how society places controls on the individual, as well as public administration, which concerns the daily operation of governments.

The newest field in political science is public policy analysis. This is the study of the decisions and actions of governments that must operate with limited resources. Examples of public policy analysis include the study of low-income housing or Welfare to Work programs.

Political scientists use many methods to obtain information. They conduct public surveys, analyze the results of elections, and interpret public documents. The discipline of political science applies statistical measures. Its researchers use computers, sometimes to manage and process extremely large amounts of data.

Careers in Political Science

Political science graduates are involved in the kinds of work for which their expertise has always been important: federal, state, and local government; law; politics; the Foreign Service; and public information. Political scientists employed by federal, state, or local governments generally specialize in one policy area. Frequently, they work with quantitative data.

Teaching and Research

About 70 percent of political scientists work in colleges and universities and are involved in teaching and research. They also do research for foundations, think tanks, and public interest groups.

Business

About 20 percent of political science graduates find employment in the business sector. After employment, some receive special training in areas including policy analysis and consumer affairs.

Labor Relations Managers

Labor relations managers are in charge of the employee relations program for the hourly workers of firms. They analyze collective bargaining agreements and assist management in developing and applying labor relations policies and practices. Labor relations managers also represent management in investigating and settling grievances. They are employed by business, industry, and consulting firms.

Politics

Some political science graduates are involved in politics as candidates, appointed officials, campaign managers, staff, or consultants.

Legislative Assistants

Legislative assistants work with legislators in preparing new legislation. They analyze policy issues and speak with lobbyists, voters, and members of the press on behalf of the legislators. They also may assist with campaign activities.

Foreign Service

Foreign Service officers represent the government of the United States in diplomatic or consular posts abroad. They also assist citizens of the United States in the host country. They are employed by the State Department.

Media

Newspapers, magazines, radio and television stations, and other media outlets employ political science graduates as analysts, political writers, and commentators.

Law

Many of those who study political science select careers in the legal profession. Lawyers conduct civil and criminal lawsuits, prepare legal documents, and advise their clients. They represent their clients in court or at government hearings.

Corporate lawyers represent large companies. They advise management of their legal rights and obligations. Probate lawyers specialize in estate settlement and planning. They draft wills and deeds of trust for their clients. Other legal specialties include family law, divorce law, environmental law, patent law, and entertainment law.

Judges administer the judicial system. They settle disputes, examine evidence, and instruct juries in laws and legal procedures. They sentence defendants in criminal cases and decide settlements in civil cases. Judges are politically appointed or elected and work in federal, state, county, and municipal governments.

Lawyers employ paralegal assistants. Paralegals belong to one of the fastest-growing professions in the United States. According to the U.S. Bureau of Labor Statistics, paralegals number more than 180,000 nationwide. Paralegal assistants research law, investigate facts, and prepare legal documents. They maintain document files and take inventory of the client's personal property in estate planning.

Related Careers

Careers related to political science include public administration, urban and regional planning, law enforcement, and legal administration. New fields opening up for political science graduates include environmental control and criminal justice and corrections.

Employment Opportunities

The greatest opportunities for political science graduates exist for those with mastery of a specialized or important policy area. The ability to work effectively with statistics, computers, data analysis, and written English is extremely valuable. Graduates may work for foundations, think tanks, and other nonprofit agencies involved in public policy.

Competition for academic positions for political scientists in colleges and universities will remain keen. Positions exist for graduates with bachelor's degrees and certification to teach government and civics in high schools.

The employment potential for labor relations managers is expected to be stable through the next decade, though union membership is declining in the United States.

Job opportunities for legislative assistants are limited. Sites of the best opportunities are in the state capitals and in Washington, D.C.

Competition for positions as Foreign Service officers is stiff. Opportunities for employment depend upon the candidate's talent, education, and determination. Applicants for these positions must first pass a competitive exam.

The job market remains highly competitive for political science graduates entering journalism and radio and television. The best opportunities for advancement are in small or medium-sized communities with a relatively small newspaper or media station.

There will continue to be some demand for lawyers, but the increased number of law school graduates is resulting in greater competition. Demand is affected by the fact that large law firms use paralegals and accountants to do some of the work that attorneys once did. The number of self-employed lawyers will decrease slowly. Prospects for establishing new law practices are best in smaller communities and suburban areas.

The hiring of government and public interest lawyers is declining due to calls for smaller and more efficient government. The best opportunities for corporate lawyers are in large metropolitan areas. Students with superior grades from the top-ranked law schools will have the best job opportunities. Some new graduates will take jobs with temporary staffing firms that place attorneys.

Job openings are expected to continue to grow for paralegals but the number of new graduates will increase also, resulting in stiff competition.

Jobs in public administration, that is, civil service jobs, in government agencies at both the federal and state levels will not show much growth due to cutbacks in government funding.

Salaries and Earnings

According to the Bureau of Labor Statistics, salaries for political scientists vary by qualifications and occupational areas but average $78,900.

The average salary of labor relations managers is $72,800 in industry and $65,500 with the federal government.

A Foreign Service officer's starting salary is $36,900 for an officer with a B.A. and no experience. It rises to $41,300 for an officer with a master's degree and no experience and $50,981 for an officer with a Ph.D.

Political scientists employed as instructors in colleges and universities earn an average starting salary of $37,500.

Paralegal assistants earn an average salary of $35,300. They earn 10 to 20 percent more for overtime work. Paralegals with the federal government average $48,500 a year. Law school graduates in private practice earn average beginning salaries ranging from $35,000 to more than $100,000 in large law firms. The national average salary for beginning government lawyers is $40,000, and for beginning corporate lawyers it is $60,000. Experienced lawyers working outside of private practice average $90,000.

Preparing for a Career in Political Science

Courses that develop essential skills such as the ability to read, write, analyze, think logically, and communicate orally are extremely beneficial. Courses in history, economics, and computer science are very useful. Since some positions with the government require fluency in a foreign language, early training is desirable.

Educational Requirements

For most careers in political science, a bachelor's degree is the minimum requirement. Some associate degree programs emphasize the knowledge, skills, and aptitudes needed for jobs and career advancement in civil service jobs.

Some paralegal assistants are trained on the job, but they are generally required to have a bachelor's degree with a paralegal certificate or to complete a two-year or four-year program in paralegal studies.

Lawyers must be graduates of law schools and be admitted to the bar. As undergraduates, they generally enroll in academic programs that involve written and oral communication skills and critical and analytical thinking. A background in social sciences, humanities, and business-related courses is strongly recommended.

Political scientists who are instructors at four-year colleges and universities generally must have a Ph.D.

Sources of Additional Information

For more information on careers in political science and allied fields, contact:

Academy of Political Science
475 Riverside Dr., Ste. 1274
New York, NY 10115
psqonline.org

American Bar Association
750 N. Lake Shore Dr.
Chicago, IL 60611
abanet.org

American Corporate Counsel Association
1025 Connecticut Ave. NW, Ste. 200
Washington, DC 20036
acca.org

American Political Science Association
1527 New Hampshire Ave. NW
Washington, DC 20036
apsanet.org

Single copies of a brochure, *Political Science: An Ideal Liberal Arts Major*, are available free from the association. A book, *Careers and the Study of Political Science: A Guide for Undergraduates*, is available for $7.00.

American Society for Public Administration
1120 G St. NW, Ste. 700
Washington, DC 20005
aspanet.org

Association of American Law Schools
Law School Admission Council
1201 Connecticut Ave. NW, Ste. 800
Washington, DC 20036
aals.org

Canadian Political Science Association
260 Dalhousie St.
Ottawa, ON K1N 7E4
cpsa-acsp.ca

Foreign Policy Association
470 Park Ave. S
New York, NY 10016
fpa.org

National Association for Law Placement
1025 Connecticut Ave. NW, Ste. 1110
Washington, DC 20036
nalp.org/prelaw/explor.htm

A brochure, *Exploring Your Career Options*, is available on its website.

National Association of Schools of Public Affairs and
    Administration
1120 G St. NW, Ste. 730
Washington, DC 20005
naspaa.org

U.S. Department of State
Office of Recruitment
HR/REE, SA-1
2401 E St. NW, 5H
Washington, DC 20522
state.gov/employment

World Policy Institute
New School University
66 Fifth Ave., 9th Fl.
New York, NY 10011
worldpolicy.org

8

ECONOMICS

ECONOMISTS STUDY THE way we allocate our resources to produce a wide variety of goods and services. In other words, economists study how we use limited resources to satisfy our wants and needs. They study the ways a society uses scarce resources, such as water, land, and fuel, to produce goods and services. They are interested in production, exchange, and consumption.

Economists investigate the causes and effects of inflation, unemployment, and taxes on our society. They collect and analyze data, monitor economic trends, and use mathematical models to develop forecasts about the economy, both in our country and overseas.

Almost all political and social problems can be described in terms of the conflict that exists between a people's unlimited desire for higher living standards and the limited resources available to satisfy this desire. Economists try to help societies, governments, and businesses resolve this conflict.

Economics is one of the older social sciences, dating back to the eighteenth century, but the discipline grew in importance after

World War II. The Great Depression of the 1930s had made governments aware that they had to find new and better ways to manage their economies.

Every day your newspaper reflects the importance of economics in our daily lives. Articles on the front page and in the business section discuss topics such as the strength or weakness of the dollar relative to other currencies, the unemployment rate, interest rates and their effects on mortgages and savings, and activity in the stock market.

Major Branches of Economics

The major branches of economics include the following:

- **Macro- and microeconomics.** Macroeconomics is the study of national and international economies. Economists in this field study such concepts as gross domestic product and monetary policy. Conversely, microeconomics studies the business firms, households, and individual consumers that make up a national economy.
- **Econometrics.** This is the most mathematical of the branches of economics. Researchers seek to measure and correlate relationships among economic variables. They use statistical methods to express economic theory.
- **International economics.** This is the comparative study of economies in various societies.
- **Labor economics.** Scholars study the place of human capital or labor in the economy.
- **Economic theory.** This is the oldest branch of economics, dating back to the beginnings of the discipline. It is the least

mathematical of the branches. Scholars address economic systems like the free market or socialism and other theories that seek to explain how economies work.

Other branches of economics include agricultural economics, environmental economics, health economics, economic history, transportation economics, and welfare economics. Applied economics includes such fields as banking, finance, insurance, and labor relations.

Careers in Economics

People who have degrees in economics work in education, business, government, and research. Only about 57 percent of all economists are employed in colleges and universities. This is a much lower percentage than in other social science fields. Approximately 32 percent work in business and 11 percent in government.

Government Economists

State and national governments and international agencies need economists to help establish public policy. Government economists help make decisions on such important policy issues as how to control inflation, how to lower unemployment, and how to design an efficient tax system. Some of the federal agencies that hire large staffs of economists are the departments of Commerce, Treasury, Labor, State, and Agriculture. Other agencies that employ many economists include the Federal Reserve System, the President's Council of Economic Advisors, the Congressional Budget Office, and the Joint Economic Committee. Economists also work in international agencies like the World Bank.

Business Economists

Business economists work in banks, trade associations, and financial services and consulting firms. Many large businesses and banks hire these economists to forecast the course of economic events.

Business economists forecast the demand for products, analyze market conditions, and supply the basic financial information that's needed for successful long-range business planning. They are employed by firms in manufacturing, transportation, and communications and by public utilities.

Teaching and Research

Jobs in universities, colleges, and research agencies challenge economics graduates to teach people the principles of economics and how to use them to solve problems. Economics professors teach both in economics departments and in business schools.

Economists in research agencies analyze economic problems, suggest ways to solve them, and try to figure out how well the solutions work. They are involved in interdisciplinary work, which ranges in scope from the economics of urban problems to redesigning the international monetary system.

Related Careers

Careers closely allied to economics include those in economic geography or geology, urban and regional planning, political science, and accounting. Those with training in economics can be employed as financial analysts, investment consultants, insurance underwriters, and budget officers.

Market research analysts are concerned with the potential sales of a product or service. They analyze data on past sales to predict future sales. They gather information on competitors and look at prices and points of distribution. They then make recommendations to their employers or to clients on the advisability of adding a new product line, opening a new store, or offering a new service.

Survey researchers design and conduct surveys to help companies and other organizations make decisions. They may ask consumers about their opinions of a product or voters about their attitudes about a candidate running for office. They use a variety of methods to collect information, including telephone and personal interviews and questionnaires sent through the mail or on the Internet.

Employment Opportunities

The employment of economists and market and survey researchers is expected to grow faster than the average for all occupations through 2010. Opportunities for economists should be best in private industry, especially in research and consulting firms, as more companies contract out economic research services. The growing complexity of the global economy, free trade, and the increased reliance on quantitative methods for analyzing business trends should increase demands for economists. Employment of economists in the federal government should decline more slowly than other federal occupations.

Demand for market research analysts should be strong because of an increasingly competitive economy. As companies look to expand their markets, the need for marketing professionals should increase. Opportunities for survey researchers should be equally strong.

Ph.D. holders in economics are likely to face keen competition for tenured positions in colleges and universities. Candidates who have state certification can become high school economics teachers. The demand for these teachers is expected to grow, as economics becomes an increasingly popular course.

Bachelor's degree holders may face competition for the limited number of jobs for which they qualify. Many graduates with bachelor's degrees will find jobs as management or sales trainees. Those with a good background in statistics, survey design, and computer science may be hired as research assistants or interviewers.

Salaries and Earnings

Because there are many opportunities for economists to work in business and finance, their salaries tend to be higher than those of other social scientists. According to the Bureau of Labor Statistics, the average salary for an economist is about $72,350. Salaries for faculty in economics departments and business schools are usually higher than those of professors in other social science departments. New assistant professors of economics earn about $47,500. Beginning salaries in the federal government for economists having a bachelor's degree average $27,200. The average salary for economists employed by the federal government is about $74,500.

Business entrants with bachelor's degrees earn about $35,000 annually. Those with master's degrees begin at about $45,000 and those with Ph.D.s at about $60,000. Economists in business average about $85,000 a year, but some business fields have much higher salaries. For example, those in the securities and investment sector average $150,000.

Preparing for a Career in Economics

Anyone considering a college major in economics should have a minimum of one year of high school algebra. A more extensive high school math background is preferred, including additional algebra and one year of plane geometry. Students should also take as many social studies courses as possible and develop strong writing skills.

Educational Requirements

To use the title of economist usually requires a graduate degree. Anyone teaching at the college or university level will need a Ph.D. A bachelor's degree in economics permits an individual to participate in entry-level training programs. For most positions, graduate training is preferred or required. Many people with bachelor's degrees in economics earn a master's degree in business administration with an emphasis in finance to work in the business world.

Sources of Additional Information

For more information about careers in economics, contact:

American Economic Association
2014 Broadway, Ste. 305
Nashville, TN 37203
vanderbilt.edu/aea

Canadian Economics Association
Department of Economics
University of Toronto
150 St. George St.
Toronto, ON M5S 3G7
economics.ca

Council of American Survey Research Organizations
3 Upper Devon
Port Jefferson, NY 11777
casro.org

Marketing Research Association
1344 Silas Deane Highway, Ste. 306
Rocky Hill, CT 06067
mra-net.org

National Association for Business Economics
1233 Twentieth St. NW, Ste. 505
Washington, DC 20036
nabe.com/careers.htm

The article "Careers in Business Economics" can be viewed at its website.

National Council on Economic Education
1212 Avenue of the Americas
New York, NY 10036
nationalcouncil.org

National Economists Club
P.O. Box 19281
Washington, DC 20036
national-economists.org

Overseas Development Council
1717 Massachusetts Ave. NW
Washington, DC 20036

9

TEACHING AND THE SOCIAL SCIENCES

ALTHOUGH THE FOLLOWING statement by an elementary school teacher could describe a teacher of any subject, it is particularly appropriate for one who chooses to teach social studies: "I shape the future. I teach."

Social studies teachers believe in the future. They teach, knowing that their influence on their students can compete successfully with other influences that shape them.

The Social Studies in Elementary, Secondary, and High Schools

Social studies is an offspring of the social sciences. In other words, the social sciences can be described as the parent discipline of social studies. Social studies is a basic subject in the elementary and secondary school curriculum. According to the National Council for the Social Studies, the professional organization for social studies teachers, social studies draws its subject matter content primarily from history, the social sciences, and, in some respects, from the humanities and science.

Classroom instruction in social studies focuses on these areas of knowledge:

- History and culture of the United States and the world
- Physical, political, economic, and cultural geography
- Theories, systems, structures, and processes of both government and economics
- The individual, group, community, and society, including intergroup and interpersonal relationships
- Global relationships between and among nations, races, cultures, and institutions

According to the National Council for the Social Studies, exemplary programs in social studies use this knowledge base to teach skills, concepts, and generalizations that can help students "understand the sweep of human affairs and ways of managing conflict consistent with democratic procedures."

In the United States there are three levels of education: elementary, secondary, and postsecondary. As you will see, the necessary skills, required educational training, and desired personal traits of the teachers at each level vary.

Teaching in the Elementary School

Elementary teachers instruct pupils in grades kindergarten through six. The educational requirements for elementary teachers are general rather than specific because they are responsible for teaching several subjects to these young students.

In most elementary schools, the teachers work with the same students during the entire school day. In some elementary schools, the teachers in grades four through six form instructional teams and divide the chief academic subjects among them. One teacher then teaches all science classes, another teaches all math classes, and then another teaches social studies to all the students enrolled in grades four, five, and six. Depending on the structure of the individual elementary school, this instructional approach is called departmentalization, or team teaching.

Effective elementary school teachers enjoy being with children. They realize that they play a critical role in their pupils' individual development. Elementary school teachers are concerned with the intellectual growth and general well-being of their pupils. They teach reading, a skill upon which most other learning depends. They are responsible for evaluating pupil progress and providing a secure learning environment. They teach as many as eight different subjects, including math, language arts, and science. One of the most important subject areas they teach is social studies.

Elementary School Social Studies

The social studies curriculum in the lower primary grades, kindergarten through grade two, draws much of its content from the disciplines of sociology and psychology. Children learn about themselves, their homes and families, and their neighborhoods. They learn about emotions such as anger and jealousy and socially acceptable ways to handle them.

In the third and fourth grades, pupils generally study their local community and state. They learn about their history, geography, government, and culture. They investigate how needs and wants are satisfied by the people who live there and how groups work together to improve the quality of life in their community and state.

In the fifth and sixth grades of elementary school, pupils learn about the United States and other countries in the world. They focus on American history and geography and examine our nation's roots in other cultures and civilizations. They learn about global awareness and worldwide interdependence.

Requirements for Teaching Elementary School Social Studies

Licensing of teachers in the United States and Canada is the responsibility of the individual states and provinces. Although certification requirements vary, an elementary school teacher is generally authorized to teach all subject areas in grades kindergarten through six. Information about each state's licensing requirements can be obtained from the teacher certification office of that state. A list of teacher certification offices of the fifty states, District of Columbia, Puerto Rico, and the American Virgin Islands is provided in Appendix A. Appendix B lists the teacher certification offices of Canada's provinces and territories.

Teaching in the Secondary School

Secondary school teachers work with pupils in grades seven through twelve. They help their students move from childhood to adulthood. Unlike elementary school teachers, who teach many subject areas to the same groups of students, secondary school teachers specialize in subject matter fields. They may teach related subjects such as American history and government, but they are supposed to be licensed in each subject area they teach.

Effective secondary school teachers enjoy working with adolescents and young adults. They not only teach their students about their areas of specialization, but they frequently also help them with personal and academic problems. Secondary school teachers interact with many students each day. An elementary school teacher may spend the day with one class of twenty to thirty students; a secondary school teacher will teach more than one hundred students each day.

Secondary School Social Studies

In most states, courses in history and geography are a requirement for high school graduation. In many states, semester-long courses in political science and, less frequently, economics are also requisites for a high school diploma. Courses in psychology, anthropology, and sociology are generally elective courses and, accordingly, few in number.

Many educated Americans deplore the low level of knowledge in history, geography, and economics among high school students. The school social studies curriculum has been the focus of several studies. The Bradley Commission issued a widely discussed report on the status of history in American schools in 1988. This commission, chaired by Kenneth Jackson, Mellon professor of history and the social sciences at Columbia University, was composed of seventeen scholars and teachers, including three Pulitzer Prize–winning historians. It harshly criticized the history curriculum in the nation's schools and called for required studies in history for students, whether or not they are preparing for college. The commission urged that history be required of all students because as citizens they will all become voters. They must, then, have an opportunity to learn American, European, and world history and geography in order to thoughtfully exercise the responsibilities of citizenship as adults.

Many scholars and educators are examining the social studies curriculum of secondary schools. There is a much greater emphasis on accountability on the part of schools. In some states, graduating seniors must take and pass a statewide exam in major subjects to receive a diploma.

Requirements for Teaching Secondary School Social Studies

During the last several years, there have been significant efforts to enhance the qualifications of teachers in the United States. Some states now require an internship for beginning teachers and the successful completion of competency exams prior to certification. Several states have abolished teacher-education majors in their state institutions. Those who intend to teach in grades seven through twelve are required to complete a baccalaureate degree in the specific discipline. For example, if someone intends to teach history in high school, a bachelor's degree in history is required.

The requirements for teacher certification are undergoing scrutiny in many states. Therefore, it is a good idea to check these requirements with the certification office of the state in which you seek employment as a teacher. Appendix A lists certification offices in the United States and Appendix B lists the teacher certification offices in Canada.

Teaching in High Schools

To be a social studies teacher requires effective oral and written communication skills and knowledge of the subject matter to be taught. Your high school preparation should include courses in English, the social sciences, and a foreign language.

It would be advantageous to join your local chapter of Future Teachers of America. You might also choose to serve as a volunteer, whereby you assist teachers in your district or tutor students having difficulty in a course in which you perform well.

If you intend to have an after-school job, try to select a position that enables you to work with people. These experiences will be valuable ones as you pursue your goal. You are, after all, intending to enter a noble profession. An ancient proverb reads: "Give a man a fish and you feed him today. Teach a man how to fish and you feed him for a lifetime." Teaching is like that. It looks to the future and attempts to empower the learner to strive for the very best.

Preparing for a Career in Teaching

All states require a baccalaureate degree for initial licensure as a teacher. In several states, additional course work or a graduate degree is required for continued certification. All studies must be completed at an accredited college or university.

A list of colleges and universities accredited by the National Council for Accreditation of Teacher Education (NCATE) can be obtained on its website at ncate.org or from:

National Council for Accreditation of Teacher Education
2010 Massachusetts Avenue NW, Suite 500
Washington, DC 20036

Certification

The interest of the American people in having their teachers certified is an old one. Even during colonial times, it was customary for public officials to examine candidates for employment as teachers. Later, the states utilized certification as a positive instrument to ensure the quality of teachers. Public officials accordingly granted different types of teaching certificates, proportioning their duration to the amount of training taken to receive them.

More recently, differentiation in the certificates issued to teachers took a different direction. Instead of certifying competence to teach for a certain length of time, the state began to certify competence in a particular field of teaching.

Such specialization in certification was evidence of the technical complexity that the professional study of education achieved in the twentieth century. By World War II, neither competence in educational technique nor mastery of subject matter was regarded as sufficient to qualify for teaching in America's schools. Rigorous rules of certification defined requirements in both. In additional to subject-matter specialization, they required courses in educational psychology and principles of education, and a specified number of hours spent in practice teaching.

However, because of teacher shortages most states allow school districts to hire uncertified teachers on special emergency licenses. After teaching for several years with a provisional license and taking education courses, these teachers can receive full certification.

On January 8, 2002, President George W. Bush signed the No Child Left Behind Act, which is intended to improve the nation's public schools. One of the provisions of the act states, "All teachers hired to teach core academic subjects must be highly qualified." This means they must have full certification, a bachelor's degree, and demonstrated competence in subject knowledge and teaching skills. Social studies is one of the core academic subjects specified by this act. Each state that receives federal Title II funds must devise a plan to ensure that all teachers of core subjects are highly qualified by the end of the 2005–2006 school year. The U.S. Department of Education estimates that nearly half the nation's middle and high school teachers don't meet these standards now. For more information on this legislation, see the U.S. Department of Education's website at nochildleftbehind.gov.

Student Teaching

In most four-year colleges, student teaching occurs near the end of the program. Student teaching programs last from eight to sixteen weeks. During that time, the student teacher works closely with an experienced teacher in the classroom. The student teacher's responsibilities gradually increase from observing, assisting, and practicing to teaching a full day. The student teacher's progress is evaluated by the classroom teacher and by a representative of the university granting the teaching degree.

Many educators regard the student teaching experience as the best predictor of the future teacher's performance. It is, in fact, the final stage of the student's undergraduate education.

To student teach, many states require a specific grade point average in college course work. In addition to knowing what to teach, secondary school teachers must also know how to help students learn. These skills are among those evaluated during the student-teaching experience.

Teacher Examinations

In most states, additional requirements must be met before prospective teachers can be certified. Chief among these additional requirements is a program of testing the prospective teachers. Tests are administered in these areas:

- **Basic skills.** Proficiency in writing, reading, spelling, and math.
- **Subject matter.** Mastery of the material to be taught.

- **Teaching skills.** Understanding of general principles of learning and education; social and cultural forces that influence curriculum and teaching; and organization and legal bases of education.

Initial Certification

Upon completion of the baccalaureate program, competency tests, and certification requirements, the candidate receives an initial teaching certificate.

In several states, the newly certified teacher must then serve a year's internship in an accredited school. The beginning teacher has a full-day teaching assignment and receives regular pay and benefits. An outstanding experienced teacher, who also has a full-time teaching assignment, serves as the beginning teacher's mentor. The mentor meets with the beginning teacher on a regular basis and provides him or her with guidance and support during the critical first year of teaching.

Subsequent Certification

Almost all states require additional education for the renewal of the teaching certificate. Many states require a graduate degree. To obtain information about the requirements for renewed certification, contact the appropriate certification officers listed in Appendixes A or B.

Additional Certification

In 1987, as a result of a recommendation in the Carnegie Corporation's report *A Nation Prepared: Teachers for the 21st Century*, the National Board for Professional Teaching Standards was established.

It has developed performance-based assessments for certifying experienced teachers who voluntarily seek recognition. Teachers are certified in specific areas, such as secondary school social studies. More than twenty-four thousand teachers have earned this certification. For further information, contact:

National Board for Professional Teaching Standards
1525 Wilson Boulevard, Suite 500
Arlington, Virginia 22209
nbpts.org

Salaries and Earnings

In the critically acclaimed report *High School: A Report on Secondary Education in America*, author Ernest Boyer states that the United States has always been ambivalent about teachers. He quotes Professor Dan Lortie of the University of Chicago, who wrote, "Teaching is honored and disdained." It is praised as "dedicated service" and lampooned as "easy work." Teaching from its beginnings has held a special, but ambiguous, social standing. Real regard shown for those who teach has never matched professed regard.

Boyer claims that the public is ambivalent about the social standing of teachers, with a large percentage of parents still preferring that their children not become teachers in U.S. public schools.

Combined with this negative public image toward teachers are other factors that have made a career in teaching a less desirable choice. Teacher salaries for the most part neither reflect the years of education needed to become a teacher nor adequately reward outstanding teachers for their performance.

It must be noted that some advances in teacher salaries are being made. Beginning teachers with a master's degree in some affluent suburban communities have starting salaries of $40,000; nonetheless, the salaries for beginning teachers today in some rural areas are less than $25,000. According to the American Federation of Teachers, beginning teachers with a bachelor's degree earned an average of $30,719 in 2001–2002. The average salary of all public school teachers in 2001–2002 was $44,367. California had the highest average salary at $54,000; South Dakota the lowest at $31,000. In some school districts, salaries for secondary school teachers are higher than those for elementary school teachers. In other districts, all teachers are on the same salary scale. More than half of all public school teachers belong to a union, which is usually affiliated with either the American Federation of Teachers or the National Education Association. This may result in higher teacher salaries. Salaries in private schools tend to be lower than those in public schools.

In many schools, teachers receive additional pay for coaching sports and working with students in extracurricular activities such as the drama club and speech teams. They may also be able to teach summer school for extra pay.

Employment Opportunities

The National Center for Education Statistics projects that the demand for teachers will increase for the immediate future. They estimate that two million new teachers will be needed by 2006. While the greatest need is for math and science teachers, there is a shortage of social studies teachers in some regions of the United States. There is also a shortage of school psychologists and school social workers. This increased need for new teachers is the result of several factors, which include changes in enrollment, changes in school policies that affect the pupil-teacher ratio, and teacher turnover or retirement.

According to the National Education Association, nearly two million teachers will retire by 2007. The National Commission on Teaching and America's Future estimates that almost one-third of all new teachers leave the classroom after three years; almost half leave after five years. Retirement is only one factor; three times as many teachers leave for other reasons. The commission is working with the states to improve teacher retention.

The American Association for Employment in Education (AAEE) has been involved in the assessment of teacher supply and demand since the early 1970s. The research reports compiled by AAEE provide accurate, valuable data for prospective teachers. Copies of the annual AAEE reports are generally available at colleges and universities; past reports are on its website at ub-careers .buffalo.edu/aaee.

Another source that will aid prospective teachers in finding a job is *Patterson's American Education*, published by Educational Directories, Incorporated. This guide identifies all school districts in the United States and lists all senior and junior high schools. It also provides the name and address of each district's superintendent. *Patterson's American Education* is revised annually and is available in many large libraries.

Teaching the Social Sciences in Colleges and Universities

College and university faculty teach undergraduate students, graduate students, or both. They prepare and give lectures in their areas of specialization and evaluate their students' progress. Faculty members in the social sciences at major universities are expected to conduct scholarly research in their fields and publish their findings. Many institutions require the publication of books and journal articles for advancement.

According to the Census Bureau, more than fourteen million full-time and part-time students are enrolled in the nation's colleges and universities. College and university faculty members hold about one million positions in these institutions. Over 75 percent of these institutions are public, that is, they are supported by the state.

Most four-year colleges require their faculty members to hold a doctoral degree for advancement. Doctoral programs require several years of full-time study beyond the bachelor's degree. They include twenty or more courses that are increasingly specialized in the area of study. A series of comprehensive examinations is also part of a doctoral program. The final stage is the successful completion of the doctoral dissertation, which is a report of original research in the field. The dissertation, completed under the guidance of a faculty adviser, usually requires several years of full-time work.

Some four-year colleges will hire a doctoral student who has completed all the course work but not the dissertation. This faculty member is frequently described as A.B.D. (all but dissertation) and is generally required to complete it during a time stipulated at employment. In two-year colleges, the doctorate is helpful but generally not required.

Tenure and Rank

An important step in a faculty member's academic career is tenure, which is intended to protect academic freedom. With tenure, a faculty member ordinarily cannot be fired. If tenure is denied, the faculty member usually must leave the institution.

Tenure is granted after a period of rigorous evaluation. New faculty members are hired generally without tenure. Only after a probationary period of up to seven years do their academic departments recommend them for tenure. This recommendation is based on a critical review of their records as teachers and researchers and their other contributions to the university.

These and other contributions made by the faculty member also determine advancement in the university. There are four levels of advancement for faculty members. Recommendations for promotion usually begin with positive evaluations by senior faculty members in the academic department.

Instructors are usually those who are hired A.B.D. They generally teach twelve to fourteen hours each week. They instruct undergraduates who are enrolled in introductory level courses.

Assistant professors usually have completed all requirements for the doctorate. They teach about twelve hours each week and frequently are responsible for larger classes of undergraduate students. They must also be involved in research and publication, especially if they hope to receive tenure.

Associate professors teach an average of nine hours each week. They are frequently assigned upper-division courses and selected graduate courses. The rank of associate professor is almost always a tenured position.

Full professors hold the highest academic rank of the faculty in a college or university. At many colleges and universities they teach only one or two classes each week. They also supervise doctoral students who are working on their dissertations. The rank of professor is difficult to attain. Increasingly promotion is based on the faculty member's research, publications, and reputation as a scholar.

Faculty Salaries

Earnings vary according to faculty rank and type of institution and, in some cases, by field. Economics professors, for example, often have higher salaries than history professors because economists have more opportunities for employment in business, finance, and government. On the average, faculty in four-year institutions earn higher salaries than those in two-year schools, and faculty in doctoral-granting universities earn more than those in colleges that only offer bachelor's degrees. According to a 2002–2003 survey by the American Association of University Professors, salaries for full-time faculty on nine-month contracts averaged $65,000. By rank, the average for professors was $86,000; associate professors, $61,700; assistant professors, $51,500; lecturers, $43,900; and instructors, $37,700.

Many faculty members augment their earnings, both during the academic year and the summer, from consulting, teaching some additional courses, research, writing for publication, or other forms of employment.

Job Outlook

According to the *Occupational Outlook Handbook*, employment of college and university faculty is expected to increase faster than the average for all occupations through the year 2010 as enrollments in higher education increase. Enrollments in institutions of higher education grew in the 1980s and 1990s, despite a decline in the traditional college-age (eighteen to twenty-four) population. This resulted from a higher proportion of eighteen- to twenty-four-year-olds attending colleges, along with a growing number of part-time, female, and older students. Enrollments are expected to continue to grow through the year 2010, particularly as the traditional college-age population increases as the baby-boom "echo" genera-tion (children of the baby boomers) reaches college age.

Openings will also occur as faculty members retire. Faculty retirements should increase significantly as the large number of fac-ulty who entered the profession during the 1960s reach retirement age. Most faculty members likely to retire are full-time tenured pro-fessors. However, in an effort to cut costs, some institutions are expected to either leave some of these positions vacant or hire part-time or temporary faculty members as replacements. Prospective job applicants should be prepared to face competition for jobs as Ph.D. graduates vie for fewer full-time tenure-track openings.

This trend of hiring adjunct or part-time faculty is likely to con-tinue due to financial difficulties faced by colleges and universities. Many states have reduced funding for higher education. As a result, colleges have increased the hiring of part-time faculty to save money on pay and benefits. Many colleges and universities are tak-ing steps to cut costs by eliminating certain academic programs, increasing class size, and closely monitoring expenses.

Sources of Additional Information

For more information about teaching careers, contact:

American Association of University Professors
1012 Fourteenth St. NW, Ste. 500
Washington, DC 20005
aaup.org

American Federation of Teachers
555 New Jersey Ave. NW
Washington DC 20001
aft.org

Canadian Association for University Teachers
2675 Queensview Dr.
Ottawa, ON K2B 8K2
caut.ca

Canadian Education Association
#300, 317 Adelaide St. W
Toronto, ON M5V 1P9
acea.ca

Consortium of Social Science Associations
1522 K St. NW, Ste. 836
Washington, DC 20005
cossa.org

National Commission on Teaching and America's Future
2010 Massachusetts Ave. NW, Ste. 201
Washington, DC 20036
nctaf.org

National Council for the Social Studies
8555 Sixteenth St.
Silver Spring, MD 20910
ncss.org

National Education Association
1201 Sixteenth St. NW
Washington, DC 20036
nea.org

Additional information regarding teaching in the social sciences is also available from the professional societies for the seven respective academic disciplines described in the earlier chapters.

10

A FINAL WORD ABOUT SOCIAL SCIENCE CAREERS

SOCIAL SCIENTISTS STUDY how people and societies interact with one another. Though the number of social scientists in the United States is not proportionately large, research in the social sciences has implications for all of us. We use the findings of the social sciences to improve our understanding of other people and their behaviors. The principles of the social sciences are all around us. We use them in many aspects of our personal and social lives. An examination of the contents of a daily newspaper can illustrate this.

- The headlines and stories on page one are frequently concerned with conflicts, wars, crime, and the economy. Principles and content from political science, history, geography, economics, and sociology are an integral part of these daily news reports.

- The classified ads list items to be bought and sold. They also list jobs available or wanted. Both these activities involve the social science of economics.
- The sports pages are more easily understood when the reader understands principles of psychology, geography, economics, and statistics.
- The travel section is concerned with geography, anthropology, and history.
- The business section deals primarily with economics.
- Sections on leisure activities frequently involve principles from sociology, anthropology, and psychology.
- The obituaries are concerned with history, sociology, and anthropology.
- The comic pages clearly involve psychology, sociology, and anthropology.

Yet many of us read the daily newspaper, not realizing that its features represent the social science disciplines.

Even if you do not choose a career in the social sciences, their study will enhance your understanding of the world around you.

Career Prerequisites

The *Occupational Outlook Quarterly* noted that there are certain requirements for those choosing careers in the social sciences. These careers require persons who have flexibility in thinking, an interest in problem solving, an ability to listen, and a willingness to ask questions.

The editors of the *Occupational Outlook Quarterly* note that the amount and time of training in the social sciences vary for different careers. Some careers require two years of college. Others require advanced graduate degrees in the appropriate field of studies. You should remember that most positions in the social sciences require at least a master's degree.

You must then be a good student who knows how to study. A strong academic program is recommended in high school. Academic competencies or broad intellectual skills are essential to work effectively in all fields of study. They are basic for success in college. The No Child Left Behind Act of 2002 will require that you undergo more standardized testing in high school, and requirements for a high school diploma in your state may be increased. This will be good preparation for college and will help you succeed as an undergraduate.

Knowledge of what is expected in college is crucial to effective learning. The College Board sells an excellent publication, *Academic Preparation for College: What Students Need to Know and Be Able to Do*. In its discussion of the competencies needed for success, the College Board states that because we live in a complex society, all people need to understand how modern societies function and how they developed. People need information concerning past civilizations and their links to present ones. If people are to perform effectively as citizens in a democratic society, they need knowledge about central institutions and values in their own society as well as in other major societies around the world. They also need to comprehend the global context of contemporary life. Defining problems and employing various kinds of information in seeking solutions to those problems require the analytical skills acquired in the study of the social sciences.

Academic Preparation for College lists and describes the knowledge and skills needed by all prospective college students. According to the College Board, the basic academic competencies are reading, writing, speaking and listening, mathematics, reasoning, and studying. These competencies or acquired skills are closely related to the basic academic subjects. Without them, learning the concepts of history, science, language, and other academic subjects is impossible.

One of the basic academic subjects taught in American high schools is social studies. Social studies combines the study of history and the social sciences and promotes skills in citizenship. The successful completion of high school courses in the social studies will prepare college entrants for advanced work in history and the social sciences, including geography, anthropology, sociology, political science, psychology, and economics.

The College Board recommends that those planning to enter college also study a foreign language. The merits of knowing another language are significant. It fosters a greater awareness of the similarities and differences among the cultures in the world. Those who know a foreign language can more readily appreciate other people's values and ways of life. Knowledge of a foreign language helps students prepare for careers in commerce, international relations, law, and the arts. College graduates need a background in another language to pursue advanced degrees in fields such as history.

If you choose to pursue a career in one of the social sciences, you should also be able to use a computer. Today it is a basic tool for acquiring and organizing information and solving problems. As such, the computer is having a profound effect on learning and the world of work.

Computers are used extensively by social scientists. People considering careers in the social sciences should have a basic knowledge of how computers work and an understanding of common computer terminology. They should be able to use appropriate software for the collection and retrieval of information and for word processing, modeling, working with simulations, running statistical tests, and decision making. They also must have some understanding of the problems and issues confronting us in the use of computers, including the social and economic effects on our lives and the ethics involved in their use.

A solid preparation in high school will be of great worth to those entering college. Courses like those described above will help the students bound for college in several important activities. Included are these:

- Gathering, assessing, and processing information
- Understanding the concepts of space and time
- Recognizing the importance of the social sciences and humanities to the past, present, and future
- Communicating and cooperating with others
- Applying problem-solving skills and critical thinking to personal and social issues

With this strong academic background from high school, you will be well prepared to begin working toward a career in the social sciences. There is, however, one other step you can take.

To help you find out if you are indeed suited for a career in the social sciences, many counselors recommend you try to get some practical work experience in a related field. The *Occupational Outlook Quarterly* suggests volunteering in hospitals, museums, schools, and libraries. Summer and part-time jobs working with people can be extremely helpful.

The Changing World of Work

Researchers have made the following projections about the U.S. economy and workforce:

- Service industries will create three-fifths of the new jobs and most of the new wealth in the future. Included in service industries are jobs in communications, finance, medical care, and social services.
- By the year 2010, 48 percent of the workforce will be made up of women. Approximately 62 percent of the women in the United States will work outside the home.
- By the year 2010, the average age of the workforce will be forty. This is seven years older than the average at any other time in U.S. history.
- The workforce will be much more ethnically and racially diverse. Minorities will make up almost one-third of the workforce.
- Employment in jobs that require a college degree is projected to grow faster than the average. These jobs will account for 42 percent of all new job growth from 2000 to 2010. Fewer well-educated workers will be available in the year 2010 than in the 1960s and 1970s; but the number of jobs requiring higher skills will increase. This may cause employers to pay those who are well educated more.

Planning for your future will enable you to survive in a changing workplace. A career is the lifelong sequence of jobs you hold. It is only one part of your life, but it has a significant impact on other life roles, such as spouse and parent. Here are four major steps you should take to advance your career development:

1. Look closely at yourself and determine your strengths.
2. Check what you find against reality.
3. Explore many options.
4. Set goals and take action.

If you follow these steps, you will make better career decisions.

Choosing a College or University

Choosing a college to attend is a major decision. It is affected by factors such as cost and distance from home. It is also affected by the perceived strengths of the school itself.

Here are some questions that you might consider when selecting a college or university:

- *Do standards vary among different colleges or schools within the same university?* For example, are the admission standards the same for those majoring in architecture as they are for those majoring in general studies? The answer can indicate how quality-conscious a program is.
- *Can students take the courses they want and need?* Limited enrollment courses can wreck students' class schedules. Lists of such courses and the number of students allowed in them are often not published. Ask about them anyway.
- *Who does the teaching?* In descending order of rank, college teachers are professors, associate professors, assistant professors, instructors, and teaching or graduate assistants. Find out how many hours teachers at different ranks spend in the classroom and whether teachers in high ranks teach freshman or survey courses. The answer can help indicate how much high-level attention students receive from faculty.

- *What is the average class size?* Find out if freshmen and sophomores enroll in small classes or if they are limited to big lecture classes.
- *How much is the library used?* This is not the same as finding out how many volumes there are in the library. Some indications of how many students do, and can, use the library are the number of study carrels assigned to undergraduates and the number reserved for seniors' use only.
- *How are computers used?* Find out if you will be expected to bring your own computer to college. Learn if computers are accessible to all students in open computer labs and how many computers are available for student use.
- *What is the success rate of recent alumni?* This is not just the number who entered law or medical school. It should include the range and median scores of undergraduates who applied to graduate schools and how many applied but did not get admitted. You should also ask about the number of graduates who are employed after graduation. Find out how long it took them to get their jobs, if they are working in jobs related to their fields, and if they are satisfied with the education they received.

Most importantly, visit the campus. After all, you may live and study there for several years. Talk with students, particularly those who are studying in the field in which you wish to major. If possible, spend a night on campus in a residence hall. Adequate pre-enrollment research will help prevent uninformed or poor decisions.

Conclusion

A career that focuses on individuals and their societies can be an extremely interesting and fulfilling one. Those who choose a career in one of the social sciences usually gain much satisfaction from their work. They find that much of what they study has implications for their own lives. Through their work they are striving to understand society and thus make a contribution to the betterment of the world.

Offices of Teacher Certification in the United States and Its Territories

Alabama

Teacher Education and Certification Office
State Department of Education
5201 Gordon Persons Bldg.
P.O. Box 302101
Montgomery, AL 36130
alsde.edu

Alaska

Coordinator of Teacher Education and Certification
State Department of Education
801 W. Tenth St., Ste. 200
Juneau, AK 99801
eed.state.ak.us/teachercertification/download.html

Arizona

Arizona Department of Education
Teacher Certification Unit
P.O. Box 6490
Phoenix, AZ 85005
ade.state.az.us/certification

Arkansas

Arkansas Department of Education
Professional Licensure
4 State Capitol Mall, Rm. 107-B
Little Rock, AR 72201
arkedu.state.ar.us/teachers

California

Commission on Teacher Credentialing
Licensing Branch
Box 944270
Sacramento, CA 94244
ctc.ca.gov

Colorado

Department of Education Teacher Certification
201 East Colfax Ave.
Denver, CO 80203
cde.state.co.us/index_license.htm

Connecticut

Bureau of Certification and Professional Development
State Department of Education
P.O. Box 150471
Hartford, CT 06115
state.ct.us/sde/dtl/cert

Delaware

Office of Certification
State Department of Education
Townsend Bldg.
P.O. Box 1402
Dover, DE 19903
deeds.doe.state.de.us

District of Columbia

Academic Credentialing and Accreditation
District of Columbia Public Schools
825 N. Capitol St. NE, 6th Fl.
Washington, DC 20002
k12.dc.us/dcps/teachdc/certification.html

Florida

Department of Education
Bureau of Teacher Certification
Turlington Bldg., Ste. 201
325 W. Gaines St.
Tallahassee, FL 32399
fldoe.org/edcert

Georgia

Certification Section
Professional Standards Commission
Two Peachtree St.
Atlanta, GA 30303
gapsc.com

Hawaii

Hawaii Teacher Standards Board
650 Iwilei Rd., #201
Honolulu, HI 96817
htsb.org

Idaho

Bureau of Certification and Professional Standards
State Department of Education
Len B. Jordan Office Bldg.
650 W. State St.
P.O. Box 83720
Boise, ID 83720
sde.state.id.us/certification

Illinois

Teacher Certification Services
Illinois State Board of Education
100 N. First St.
Springfield, IL 62777
isbe.net/teachers

Indiana

Professional Standards Board
101 W. Ohio St., Ste. 300
Indianapolis, IN 46204
state.in.us/psb

Iowa

Board of Educational Examiners
Department of Education
Grimes State Office Bldg.
Des Moines, IA 50310
state.ia.us/boee

Kansas

Teacher Education and Licensure
State Department of Education
120 SE Tenth Ave.
Topeka, KS 66612
ksde.org/cert/cert.html

Kentucky

Division of Certification
Education Professional Standards Board
State Department of Education
1024 Capitol Center Dr., Ste. 225
Frankfort, KY 40601
kyepsb.net/cert/default.html

Louisiana

Division of Teacher Standards, Assessment, and Certification
Teacher Certification and Higher Education
P.O. Box 94064
Baton Rouge, LA 70804
doe.state.la.us/lde/tsac/home.html

Maine

Teacher Certification and Placement
Certification Office
23 State House
Augusta, ME 04333
state.me.us/education/cert/cert.htm

Maryland

State Department of Education
Certification Branch
200 W. Baltimore St.
Baltimore, MD 21201
certification.msde.state.md.us

Massachusetts

Office of Certification and Teacher Credentialing
Massachusetts Department of Education
350 Main St.
Malden, MA 02148
doe.mass.edu/educators/e_license.html

Michigan

Office of Professional Preparation and Certification
State Department of Education
P.O. Box 30008
Lansing, MI 48909
michigan.gov/mde

Minnesota

Personnel Licensing
State Department of Education
1500 Highway 36 W
Roseville, MN 55113
education.state.mn.us

Mississippi

Office of Teacher Certification
State Department of Education
P.O. Box 771
Jackson, MS 39205
mde.k12.ms.us/license

Missouri

Director of Teacher Certification
P.O. Box 480
Jefferson City, MO 65102
dese.state.mo.us/divteachqual/teachcert

Montana

Educator Licensure Unit
Office of Public Instruction
State Capitol
P.O. Box 202501
Helena, MT 59620
opi.state.mt.us

Nebraska

Teacher Education and Certification
State Department of Education
301 Centennial Mall S
P.O. Box 94987
Lincoln, NE 68509
nde.state.ne.us/tcert/tcmain.html

Nevada

Teacher Licensure Office
State Department of Education
1820 E. Sahara Ave., Ste. 205
Las Vegas, NV 89104
nde.state.nv.us/licensure/nbpts/index.html

New Hampshire

Bureau of Credentialing
State Department of Education
State Office Park South
101 Pleasant St.
Concord, NH 03301
ed.state.nh.us/certification/teacher.htm

New Jersey

Office of Licensing and Academic Credentials
Department of Education
3535 Quakerbridge Rd.
CN 503
Trenton, NJ 08625
state.nj.us/njded/educators/license/index.html

New Mexico

Professional Licensure Unit
Department of Education
Education Bldg.
Santa Fe, NM 87501
sde.state.nm.us/divisions/ais/licensure

New York

Office of Teaching Initiatives Certification Unit
Department of Education
5N Education Bldg.
Albany, NY 12234
highered.nysed.gov/tcert

North Carolina

Division of Certification
Department of Public Instruction
301 N. Wilmington St.
Raleigh, NC 27601
ncpublicschools.org/employment.html

North Dakota

Education Standards and Practices Board
State Department of Public Instruction
State Capitol Bldg., 9th Fl.
600 E. Boulevard Ave.
Bismarck, ND 58505
state.nd.us/espb

Ohio

Office of Certification/Licensure
State Department of Education
25 S. Front St., Mail Stop 105
Columbus, OH 43215
ode.state.oh.us/teaching-profession/teacher/certification_licensure

Oklahoma

Professional Standards Section
State Department of Education
2500 N. Lincoln Blvd., #212
Oklahoma City, OK 73105
sde.state.ok.us/pro/tcert/profstd.html

Oregon

Teachers Standards and Practices Commission
465 Commercial St., NE
Salem, OR 97301
tspc.state.or.us

Pennsylvania

Department of Education
Bureau of Teacher Certification
333 Market St.
Harrisburg, PA 17126
pde.state.pa.us

Puerto Rico

Teacher Certification Division
Department of Education
Box 759
Hato Rey, PR 00919

Rhode Island

Department of Elementary and Secondary Education
Shepard Bldg.
255 Westminster St.
Providence, RI 02903
ridoe.net/teacher_cert

South Carolina

Teacher Quality
State Department of Education
Landmark II Office Bldg., Ste. 500
3700 Forest Dr.
Columbia, SC 29204
scteachers.org/cert/index.cfm

South Dakota

Office of Accountability and Teacher Certification
Department of Education
700 Governors Dr.
Pierre, SD 57501
state.sd.us/deca/opa

Tennessee

Office of Teacher Licensing
State Department of Education
Andrew Johnson Tower, 5th Fl.
710 James Robertson Pkwy.
Nashville, TN 37243
state.tn.us/education/lic_home.htm

Texas

State Board for Educator Certification
Texas Education Agency
4616 W. Howard La., Ste. 120
Austin, TX 78728
sbec.state.tx.us/sbeconline

Utah

Educator Licensing
State Office of Education
250 E. 500 S
P.O. Box 144200
Salt Lake City, UT 84114
usoe.k12.ut.us/cert

Vermont

Certification Division
Licensing Office
State Department of Education
120 State St.
Montpelier, VT 05620
state.vt.us/educ/license

Virgin Islands

Educational Personnel Services
Department of Education
44-46 Kongens Gade
St. Thomas, VI 00802

Virginia

Division of Teacher Education and Licensure
State Department of Education
P.O. Box 2120
Richmond, VA 23218
pen.k12.va.us/vdoe/newvdoe/teached.html

Washington

Professional Education and Certification Office
Office of the Superintendent of Public Instruction
Old Capitol Bldg.
Olympia, WA 98504
k12.wa.us/cert

West Virginia

Office of Professional Education
State Department of Education
1900 Kanawha Blvd. East
Charleston, WV 25305
wvde.state.wv.us/certification

Wisconsin

Bureau of Teacher Education, Professional Development, and
  Licensing
State Department of Public Instruction
Drawer 794
Milwaukee, WI 53293
dpi.state.wi.us/dpi/dlsis/tel/licguide.html

Wyoming

Professional Teaching Standards Board
State Department of Education
1920 Thomes Ave., Ste. 400
Cheyenne, WY 82001
k12.wy.us/ptsb/certification.htm

Appendix B

Offices of Teacher Certification in Canadian Provinces and Territories

Alberta

Alberta Learning
Communication Branch
Commerce Pl., 7th Fl.
10155-102 St.
Edmonton, AB T5J 4L5
learning.gov.ab.ca/k_12/teaching/certification

British Columbia

British Columbia College of Teachers
400-2025 W. Broadway
Victoria, BC V6J 1Z6
bcct.ca/certification.html

Manitoba

Professional Certification Unit
P.O. Box 700, 402 Main St.
Russell, MB R0J 1W0
edu.gov.mb.ca/ks4/profcert

Newfoundland and Labrador

Department of Education
Registrar of Teacher Certification
P.O. Box 8700
St. John's, NF A1B 4J6
gov.nf.ca/edu/k12/tcert.htm

Northwest Territories and Nunavut

Department of Education, Culture, and Employment
P.O. Box 1320
Yellowknife, NT X1A 2L9
siksik.learnnet.nt.ca

Nova Scotia

Department of Education
Teacher Certification Board
P.O. Box 578
Halifax, NS B3J 2S9
certification.ednet.ns.ca/index.shtml

Ontario

Ontario College of Teachers
121 Bloor St. E, 6th Fl.
Toronto, ON M4W 3M5
oct.ca

Prince Edward Island

Department of Education
P.O. Box 2000
Charlottetown, PE C1A 7N8
edu.pe.ca/registrar/certappl.asp

Québec

Ministère de l'Éducation
1035 rue De La Chevrotière, 28e étage
Québec, QC G1R 5A5
meq.gouv.qc.ca

Saskatchewan

Provincial Examinations, Student, and Teacher Services
Saskatchewan Learning
1500-4th Ave.
Regina, SK S4P 3V7
sasked.gov.sk.ca/student_records/certificationprocedures.htm

Yukon Territory

Department of Education
P.O. Box 2703
Whitehorse, YT Y1A 2C6
gov.yk.ca/depts/education

Selected Professional Journals in the Social Sciences

Anthropology

American Anthropologist
American Antiquity
American Ethnologist
American Journal of Archaeology
American Journal of Physical Anthropology
Anthropological Linguistics
Archaeology
Current Anthropology
Journal of Field Archaeology
Language
Language in Society

Sociology

Ageing International
American Journal of Sociology
American Sociological Review
Gerontologist
Journal of Family Issues
Journal of Marriage and the Family
Rural Sociology
Social Forces
Social Problems
Social Work
Sociological Quarterly
Sociology of Education

Psychology

American Journal of Psychology
American Psychologist
Educational Psychologist
Journal of Applied Psychology
Journal of Consulting and Clinical Psychology
Journal of Counseling Psychology
Journal of Educational Psychology
Journal of Experimental Psychology
Journal of School Psychology
Professional School Counseling
Psychology in the Schools

History

American Archivist
American Heritage
American Historical Review
Historian: A Journal of History
The Historical Journal
The History Teacher
Journal of American History
Journal of Popular Culture
Magazine of History: For Teachers of History
Preservation
Public Historian

Geography

American Planning Association Journal
Cartography and Geographic Information Science
Environment and Planning
Geographical
Geographical Review
Journal of Cultural Geography
Journal of Geography
Mercator's World
Planning
Urban Geography

Political Science

ABA Journal
American Journal of Political Science
American Political Science Review
Current History
Foreign Affairs
Foreign Policy
Journal of Politics
Law and Contemporary Problems
National Law Journal
Policy Studies Journal
Political Science Quarterly
World Affairs

Economics

American Economic Review
Contemporary Economic Policy
Economic History Review
Economic Journal
The Economist
International Economic Review
Journal of Cultural Economics
Journal of Economic Education
Journal of Economic Literature
Review of Economic Studies
Review of Economics and Statistics
World Bank Research Observer

Resources

Academic Preparation for College: What Students Need to Know and Be Able to Do. New York: The College Board, 1983.

Boyer, Ernest L. *High School: A Report on Secondary Education in America.* New York: Harper and Row, 1983.

Camenson, Blythe. *Great Jobs for Anthropology Majors.* Lincolnwood, IL: VGM Career Books, 1999.

————. *Great Jobs for Economics Majors.* Lincolnwood: VGM Career Books, 2000.

Canadian Almanac and Directory. Toronto: Micromedia ProQuest, 2003.

DeGalan, Julie, and Stephen Lambert. *Great Jobs for History Majors,* 2d ed. Lincolnwood: VGM Career Books, 2001.

————. *Great Jobs for Psychology Majors,* 2d ed. Lincolnwood: VGM Career Books, 2000.

Jackson, Kenneth, chair. *The Bradley Commission on History in the Schools: Building a History Curriculum.* Washington: Educational Excellence Network, 1988.

Lambert, Stephen. *Great Jobs for Sociology Majors*, 2d ed. Chicago: VGM Career Books, 2002.

Rowh, Mark. *Great Jobs for Political Science Majors*. Lincolnwood, IL: VGM Career Books, 1998.

Super, Charles M., and Donald E. Super. *Opportunities in Psychology Careers*. Lincolnwood: VGM Career Books, 2001.

United States Department of Labor. *Occupational Outlook Handbook*, 2002–2003. New York: McGraw-Hill, 2002.

Wittenberg, Renee. *Opportunities in Social Work Careers*. Chicago: VGM Career Books, 2003.

About the Author

Rosanne J. Marek is chair of the Department of History at Ball State University in Muncie, Indiana. She received her doctorate from Kent State University and her Master of Science degree from the University of Dayton. She teaches undergraduate students in survey courses in American and world history as well as pre-service social studies teachers. Prior to coming to Ball State, she taught in a number of elementary schools in Ohio.

For several years Dr. Marek worked with Ball State students who had not yet selected a major. She established the university's Learning Center and served as its director for two years.

She is a past president of the Indiana Association for Developmental Education and a member of the Awards Committee of the National Council for the Social Studies. She is a member of several organizations, including the Organization of American Historians, Indiana Council for the Social Studies, National Council for History Education, National Council for Geographic Education, and American Historical Association.